BECAUSE OF ROMEK

A HOLOCAUST SURVIVOR'S MEMOIR

BY DAVID FABER

With Anna Vaisman
&
James D. Kitchen

BECAUSE OF ROMEK
A HOLOCAUST SURVIVOR'S MEMOIR
-2ND EDITION-

Paperback ISBN 0-9768763-0-2
Hardcover ISBN 0-9768763-1-0

Faber Press
5638 Lake Murray Blvd., #206
La Mesa, CA 91942-1929

Cover by Daryl Rysdyk.

Printed in the United States of America   15   14   13   12

Publishing History:
Because of Romek, by David Faber with James D. Kitchen. Los Hombres Press, 1990,
LCCN: 90-84347, ISBN 0-9623497-8-X.
Because of Romek: A Holocaust Survivor's Memoir. Granite Hills Press ™ 1997-2001,
LCCN: 96-79651, ISBN 0-9638886-2-5.
Because of Romek: A Holocaust Survivor's Memoir. Vincent Press Publishing Co. 2003-2004,
 LCCN: 2003108074, ISBN 0-9728077-0-5.
German Translation:
Romeks Bruder. Erinnerungen eines Holocaust-Überlebenden, published by Deutscher Taschenbuch
Verlag (dtv), Munich, Germany, 2000, ISBN 3-423-30761-7

www.BECAUSEofROMEK.com

SAN 256 – 8071
Faber Press
5638 Lake Murray Blvd., #206
La Mesa, CA 91942-19299

Phone: 619-517-2662
Fax: 619-255-2354

PUBLISHER'S CATALOGING IN PUBLICATION

Faber, David.
  Because of Romek: a Holocaust Survivor's Memoir, 2nd Edition / by David Faber with
Anna Vaisman and James D. Kitchen – Faber Press.
   p. cm.
  Library of Congress Control Number: 2005928907
  Paperback ISBN 0-9768763-0-2
  Hardcover ISBN 0-9768763-1-0

ABRAHAM FABER (nicknamed ROMEK) [photo c. 1937],David's older brother, is wearing the uniform of the Polish army, including a medal (lower right). Romek was tortured to death at about age 27 in Gestapo headquarters in Tarnów, Poland, 1942 (Chapters 1 and 12). It was Romek's memory that inspired David Faber to write this book, thus the title: *Because of Romek.*

PRAISE BY EDUCATORS

"*Because of Romek* is required reading in my combined English and World History class, where we study it as living history and as literature. It is the highlight of our school year."

—Michael Corle, teacher, grades 9-12
University City High School, San Diego, CA

"Reading *Because of Romek* was a traumatic experience for me, but I couldn't put it down. I teach psychology to students from all over the world, and I ask my students, 'How could people do such things?' I urge them to read David Faber's book as an inoculation against such cruelty to humans by humans ever happening again."

—Dr. James McCarthy
San Diego Community College

"I overhear my students asking one another, 'Have you finished *Because of Romek* yet? May I have it next?' This book makes history come alive for them."

—Ellie Taylor, teacher, grade 8
Bernardo Heights Middle School, San Diego, CA

"I teach history and geography to students with troubled backgrounds. They are inspired by David Faber's book. It is a guide to them. He makes them believe that if he could make it, so can they.

—Joyce Levine, teacher, grades 9-12
Chaparral High School, El Cajon, CA

"David Faber's book with all its pain and struggle for survival, ends up teaching that love is more powerful than hate. This is a major lesson of my religion class."

—Dr. John Gillman
San Diego State University
Chaplain, Mercy Hospital

DEDICATION

To the memory of my entire family

PUBLISHER'S PREFACE 2005

FABER PRESS is proud to publish the second edition of *Because of Romek: A Holocaust Survivor's Memoir*. New to this edition are more photos, as well as an expanded notes section that includes glossary terms and extensive historical research. All of David Faber's story remains intact. However, some new text has been added to the existing narrative, and some of the narrative is expanded upon in more detail. There is also a new introduction by Anna Vaisman, who co-authored this edition many years after having written the poem "Final Solution" that has appeared in the book since its first printing in 1990.

PUBLISHER'S PREFACE 2001

New to this sixth printing of *Because of Romek: A Holocaust Survivor's Memoir* by David Faber are three photographs of Mrs. Crosthwaite and Mrs. Montgomery, the British Red Cross volunteers who rescued David Faber at Bergen-Belsen Concentration Camp and later helped him find his sister Rachel in London. We thank Mr. and Mrs. John Collinson, relatives of Mrs. Montgomery, and Sir David and Lady Melanie Landale, relatives of Mrs. Crosthwaite, for providing the photographs and for granting permission to print them.

Also new to this printing is an expanded discussion of the location of Krawinkel Concentration Camp (see References and Notes, Chapter 21). We thank Brigitte Hellmann of Deutscher Taschenbuch Verlag (dtv) for her contribution to the Krawinkel research.

The text of the book is unchanged from the 1999 printing.

Deutscher Taschenbuch Verlag (dtv), Munich, published the German translation in 2000 under the title *Romeks Bruder. Erinnerungen eines Holocaust-Überlebenden.*

PUBLISHER'S PREFACE 1999

In 1997, Deutscher Taschenbuch Verlag (dtv), Munich, Germany, requested and received the rights to translate *Because of Romek: A Holocaust Survivor's Memoir* by David Faber, published by Granite Hills Press™, into German and to publish it under the title *Romeks Bruder. Erinnerungen eines Holocaust-Überlebenden*, in press. We thank the staff at dtv for making this work accessible to the German-speaking audience. We thank the translator Gabriele Ackermann and other consultants at dtv for identifying areas in the text that needed clarification.

Attempts at clarification led us to further investigation of dates, places, and other details in published references. We found extensive evidence to support Faber's account of incidents such as the Nazis' burning people alive and places such as an almost unheard-of camp called Krawinkel. The highlights of this research are included in the References and Notes. In a few instances, conflicts existed between Faber's memory and the published record, usually concerning a date or the exact location of an area within a particular camp. In those cases, Faber deferred to the record, and a few corresponding changes have been made in this printing, such as providing his recorded date of arrival at Auschwitz, and deleting the duplication of the Auschwitz motto at Buchenwald. None of the changes has any material effect on Faber's narrative.

In our search for the relevant references, we were aided by and we thank many scholars including Dr. Jonathan Friedman, Historian, Survivor's of the Shoah

Visual History Foundation, Los Angeles, CA, and Dr. Steven Luckert, Curator of the Permanent Exhibit, United States Holocaust Memorial Museum, Washington, DC. We are especially indebted to Mr. Steven Vitto, Reference Librarian, United States Holocaust Memorial Museum, Washington, DC, who found David Faber's exact date of arrival at Auschwitz and the locations of Pustkow, Szebnia, and Krawinkel, the lesser known concentration camps. Mr. Vitto also brought to our attention several invaluable references that are included in the Bibliography.

We also thank Mrs. Veronica Marchbanks, Archives Assistant, British Red Cross, London, England, who researched the war records, corrected the spelling of names, and located the living relatives of Mrs. Crosthwaite and Mrs. Montgomery, the British Red Cross nurses who rescued David Faber at Bergen-Belsen and helped him find his sister Rachel in England.

We are indebted to the late Leo Wachtel, husband of Rachel Faber Wachtel, who gave Rachel's prewar family photographs to Faber after Rachel died. These are included in the Photographs section. They are David Faber's sole photographs of his birth family.

PUBLISHER'S PREFACE 1997

Granite Hills Press™ is honored to be the new publisher of *Because of Romek* by David Faber. This first Granite Hills Press™ edition of Faber's moving, autobiographical record of the Holocaust and World War II is the same in every essential way as previous editions. The differences are these:

Elements that the author had intended for publication but which were omitted from previous editions, such as the names of all six of his sisters and several incidents in the narrative, were restored.

Typographical errors were corrected. The spelling of the names of concentration camps, foreign cities and streets, foreign language dialogue, and the customary spelling found in historical documents and records. The following experts and institutions provided invaluable help:

Language editors: German—Jutta Bailey, San Diego State University; Italian—Serena Anderlini-D'Onofrio, San Diego State University; Russian—Anna Shapiro and Susan K. Larsen, University of California, San Diego; English—Rebecca Rauff, freelance editor, Decatur, Illinois.

Research facilities: United States Holocaust Memorial Museum Research Institute; Simon Wiesenthal Center Library & Archives; Embassy of the Federal Republic of Germany, Washington, DC; Polish Cultural Center, NY; The Kosciuszko Foundation, Inc., NY; Slavic Reference Service, University of Illinois; Embassy of Great Britain, Washington, DC; British Red Cross, London; and the personal documents of David Faber.

Granite Hills Press™ thanks Marina Kagan for laser typesetting this edition and Lina Faber for her unwavering encouragement to her author-husband.

Because of Romek fulfills the promise the author made to his dead mother to "tell the world." *Because of Romek* provides educators with a clear and meaningful tool for teaching about the horrors of the past so future generations will not repeat them. *Because of Romek* honors the dead and teaches the living.

Judith S. Rubenstein, Ed.D., Former Publisher (1997-2004)

CONTENTS

INTRODUCTION

I was fourteen years old when David Faber first came into my life by marrying my grandmother, Lina. I was a year older than David had been when he was sent to the first of many concentration camps. When he asked me to coauthor this second edition of **Because of Romek**, I was of course honored but also somewhat apprehensive. I knew that I would have to go back and reread all the horrors that he had to endure. Some people have asked me whether it was difficult to write about all the unthinkable things that happened to someone I know and love. Of course it was a challenge. I read the prior edition of the book once more and spent many days staring at my computer screen through tear-soaked eyes.

After many months of researching and writing, I am left with the same questions that many people have asked David over the years. How did he survive? How did he maintain his faith in God? He has told me his answer to these questions, yet I am still amazed.

The answer is that he is not sure himself. After all, he had many chances to die, yet he did not. He had a multitude of opportunities to be killed in all sorts of horrible and painful ways, yet he lived. He even considered killing himself on several occasions, yet he did not. It seems that three things kept him going: his ability to speak several languages, including fluent German, his survival instinct, and the promise he made to his dead mother to survive and tell the world what happened. As for maintaining his faith in God, David has said on numerous occasions that he did not have any faith for many years. After suffering so much torture, starvation, pain, and especially the murder of his family, he lost his faith – as was common with many Holocaust survivors. However, he also always said that he regained his faith when he met my grandmother and was embraced by our family.

It is a strange fate that this man, whom I have called my grandfather for so many years now and who is a member of our large family, lost his own family at such a young age. After working on the grim details of his story for the past two years, I am not at all sure that I would have been as strong as he under the same circumstances. It is frightening to think about it.

It is perhaps equally frightening to consider the fact that the Holocaust was not an isolated incident in the world – there have been many Holocausts throughout human history, and genocidal atrocities continue to occur in various tumultuous corners of the world today.

This new edition includes many never-before published items. Over the years that I have known David Faber, he has told me so much more than what was included in the earlier edition of the book. We tried to fill in the gaps of previously incomplete stories, as well as include more pictures and historical research.

We owe special thanks to the many organizations and individuals who contributed their time, energy, knowledge, and research to make this second edition possible, including Yad Vashem, U.S. Holocaust Memorial Museum, U.S. National Archives and Records Administration, Simon Wiesenthal Center, Gedenkstatte Bergen-Belsen, the International Committee of the Red Cross, Grzegorz Szczerba, Rebecca Wallach, Philipp Wulf, and many others. Special thanks also to my family, especially my husband, for all their support, encouragement, and patience. Very special thanks to David Faber, a truly amazing individual. To help prevent anything on the scale of the Holocaust of World War II from ever happening again and to maintain his promise to his mother, David asked me to promise him that I would keep his story alive. I am doing my best to keep my word.

Anna Vaisman
July 2005

FINAL SOLUTION

Smoke droops low
Blackening all it touches;
Flames eat away
All in their path.
The small room shrinks,
Suffocating,
Sucking last breaths from life.
Outside, sounds seep through the walls,
But voices are muffled.
All that is clearly heard
Is crackling fire
That turns life to ashes.

Let me paint you my picture,
Though you may not like it.
Let me scream out the truth,
Though you may not believe it.
I shall prove you wrong,
Though you may not want it.
But the truth shall be known,
For there are survivors.

—Anna Vaisman
Granddaughter of David Faber
Age 16

PROLOGUE

KATOWICE *The War Begins*

Poland. Late August, 1939. I heard planes circling low over my hometown of Katowice.[1] All day their loudspeakers blared assurances. "We are strong. If the Germans come, we will stop them. Don't panic! We are strong!" No one believed it.

German armored panzer divisions[2] struck at the Polish city of Pszczyna. Polish defenses crumbled. Hundreds of our soldiers died; thousands more went to POW camps.

From our third-floor apartment on the street *ulica*[3] *Pocztowa*, I watched German army trucks loaded with steel-helmeted men in grey uniforms. Like messengers of death, the Nazis had come.

Life was hard before in a city where most people were German—and Catholic. A crucifix hung in every school room, and the days began and ended with students kneeling in prayer. We Jewish children didn't kneel, and the other children called us "Christ killers."

Home was a refuge from the mocking and bullying. Papa's quiet presence gave me courage; my six sisters, Rachel, Kreindel, Laika, Fella, Sabina, and Sonia, and my brother Romek, all older, alternately pampered and teased me; and Mama's love warmed us all.

Papa imported lemons and oranges from other countries and sold them to fruit stores, but it was Mama who made the business go. She spoke several languages. The synagogue[4] was the center of Papa's life, and he went there every morning, noon, and evening.

What would happen now? I'd heard stories from Jews who had fled from Hitler. People lost their jobs, their shops. Others disappeared overnight, and no one heard from them again. That would happen in Katowice, I knew. Papa's faith couldn't save us, nor Mama's love.

CHAPTER ONE

Romek *A Startling Revelation*

My own scream cut through my sleep and shattered the horror of seeing Romek die again. I felt a hand on my shoulder; a voice comforted me. "It's all right, David, it's all right," my wife Tonya said. "We're safe now."

I sat up, rubbed my face, and patted Tonia's hand. "I know. I haven't dreamed about it for years. The letter brought it back."

I couldn't get the letter out of my mind. I knew Romek was dead. Nothing could bring him back. The Germans had killed him, and now they were stirring it up again. Why couldn't they leave it alone? Tonia had given me the envelope when I came home from work the day before. Anger filled me when I read the return address, "Consulate General of the Federal Republic of Germany." My fingers trembled as I tore the heavy paper and pulled out the letter. "We have matters of importance," it said. "We would like you to be a witness in the case of your brother, Abraham Faber. We would appreciate it if you would meet us in New Haven, Connecticut at the Hilton Hotel...."

My brother's name was Abraham, but his Polish nickname was Romek.

I looked at my wife. "I wonder what's going on? This is 1966! What do they want?"

"Why don't you call and find out?" she said. "I don't think you should go to meet them or agree to be a witness until you know about it."

I picked up the telephone and dialed the number on the letterhead. "This is David Faber. I would like to speak with Dr. von Keudell."[1]

A few seconds later, a man said in German, "*Jawohl.*"

"Dr. von Keudell, I would like to speak in English. I speak German, but I prefer English."

"Whatever you wish."

"My name is David Faber. I received a letter from you asking me to testify in a case concerning my brother, Abraham Faber. I don't understand. You Germans tortured him to death. What more do you want from him or me?"

"I'm sorry, but I can't tell you more until you meet with us."

"Look, Dr. von Keudell, I'm also sorry, but I have no intention of becoming involved in something I know nothing about. I won't go to New Haven or anywhere else until you tell me what you're up to. I just don't trust you."

"We very much need your help. I'm sorry I can't tell you more."

"If you can't, I refuse to do anything," I said and hung up the phone.

I turned to my wife. "I hope that's the end of it."

But it wasn't. A week later, there was a phone call from a man who said he was with the FBI.

"We would appreciate it if you would cooperate with the German government," he told me.

"Cooperate about what?" I responded. "They won't tell me anything. I don't even know who *you* are or if you're really from the FBI. I'm not doing anything without more information."

The next day, I answered a knock at the front door. A man stood there, dressed in a business suit and wearing a hat.

"Mr. David Faber?" he asked.

"Yes. Who are you?"

He held out a leather case with a card that said FBI and had his picture and name on it. "Here are my credentials," he said. "May I come in and talk to you?"

"Yes, come in. But I've already talked to the FBI on the telephone. I told them I couldn't help unless they told me what this is all about."

He stepped into the house but remained standing.

"Did you talk to Dr. von Keudell at the German Consulate?" he asked.

"Yes. I told him the same thing I told the FBI."

"It's very important that you cooperate with the Germans in this matter. It's important to the United States also."

"Look, sir," I said, "the Germans did so many terrible things to me and to my family. Do you expect me to trust them, to be alone in a roomful of Germans, and I don't even know why? It's too dangerous. I won't do it."

He tried to persuade me, but I interrupted. "Do you know how they killed my brother, how I saw them torture him to death right in front of me? I'm sorry, but you're wasting your time here."

After another thirty minutes or so of reasons why I should meet with the Germans and my repeated refusals to do so, the FBI man finally left.

The same scene was repeated about a week later, this time with another agent. Again I spoke of the horrors the Germans had brought to me and my family, and I demanded at least some hint of what they wanted now, and again my demand was refused.

"You'll find out when you get there" was the only response.

Around noon on my day off a week later, the telephone rang. When I answered, a man spoke to me in Yiddish.[2]

"This is Senator Jacob Javits,"[3] he said. "Am I speaking to Mr. David Faber?"

"Yes, sir."

He went on, telling me how important it was for both the American and the German governments to ask me questions about my brother and urging me to meet with them.

"But how can I tell them anything they don't know?" I asked. "I was only a boy, and I didn't know what my brother did when he was away from the ghetto. I don't know anything, and I don't want to see those people again. Why don't they leave me alone? Haven't they done enough to me and my family? Nothing I can tell them can help Romek, anyway. He's been dead for twenty-five years. And how do I know you're the person you say you are, that you really are Senator Jacob Javits?"

"I can't tell you any more on the telephone," he said. "But this matter is so important that I'll meet with you, and then I can tell you about it."

"Can you come to Springfield, Massachusetts?" I asked him.

"How about this Friday?" he asked.

"Yes, I can arrange to do that," I said. "Can you meet me at the Beth El synagogue?"

"I'll meet you there at noon," he said. "You'll feel safe there, and we can talk."

"Thank you, sir. I will be there."

I was still confused and uneasy about the whole matter, but meeting in a synagogue with someone who claimed to be Jacob Javits seemed safe enough. So I went to the Beth El synagogue that Friday.

When I went up the steps and through the front door, a man stepped toward me. "The senator is waiting for you," he said, and waved toward the front of the sanctuary.

I looked up. Yes, it was Jacob Javits. I recognized him at once from the many times I had seen him on television and in newspaper pictures. I hurried down the aisle toward him.

We shook hands and he thanked me for coming. "I have only a few minutes," he said, "so I'll tell you as quickly as possible. Your brother was a member of a large underground unit carrying out sabotage against the Nazis. Among other things, they destroyed shipments of heavy water[4] into Germany, and without that the Nazis couldn't build an atomic bomb."

I interrupted. "I'm sorry, sir, but I knew nothing about it. I was just a boy and had nothing to do with the underground. Besides, how can any of this help Romek?"

The senator held up his hand. "It's a matter of seeing justice done. Your brother and his group saved many lives before he died, before he was betrayed by a double agent. For years, both we and the Germans have looked for that man, and now we think we've found him. Maybe you can help us prove it."

"How? I don't know anything about it!"

"Why don't you let us make that decision? Why don't you go talk with the Germans? For your brother's sake."

"I'm still afraid to be alone in a room with Germans," I said. "How can I be sure it's safe?"

"You won't be alone," Javits said. "The FBI man who came to see you will be in the room. You have my word."

Tears came to my eyes. In my mind, Romek's agony was as sharp and terrible as when he suffered it. Now I knew why the Gestapo had wanted him to talk and why he had chosen death instead.

"Yes," I barely whispered. "I will go. I will do anything I can."

"Thank you, David." Senator Javits shook my hand and walked out of the synagogue.

One week later, I boarded a Greyhound bus for New Haven, Connecticut. As I entered the lobby of the Hilton Hotel in that city, a short, chubby man approached me.

"*Herr* Faber? *Herr* David Faber?"

The heavy German accent took me back to the camps and the horror. My body felt chilled, and for a moment I couldn't speak.

"There's no reason to be afraid," I told myself. "This is America." I forced myself to answer.

"Yes, I am David Faber."

"Please come upstairs. The others are waiting."

We entered the elevator and rose to the third floor, where another man greeted us as we walked into the hallway.

"Gentlemen," he said, "please come in." He led the way into a room directly opposite the elevator. A tall, dark-haired man with a scar on one cheek stepped from the group gathered there and held out his right hand.

"I am Dr. von Keudell, Mr. Faber. We spoke on the telephone."

"Yes," I replied, hesitating before shaking hands. I was uneasy among all these Germans. Where was the FBI man Javits had promised? Ah, there he was on the far side of the room. There was nothing to be afraid of.

Some other Germans came forward and introduced themselves as officers of the German court.

"I would like to ask you some questions," one of them said, a tall, heavy man with a deep voice. "But first, I'd like to show you something."

"All right."

He pulled a sheaf of papers and some photographs from a brown, leather briefcase.

"Please look at this picture." He handed me a large photograph. "Do you recognize the place?"

As I looked at the photo, bitter memories flooded my mind. I could almost smell the fear I had smelled then. I closed my eyes for a moment. "It's Jews' Street, ulica Zydowska in Tarnów."

U.S. Senate Historical Office

SENATOR JACOB JAVITS (NY)

"Please, look at a second one."

"And the third one, please. Have you seen that man before?"

"I've seen him before. How could I forget? That's the murderer, Grunow. *Hauptsturmführer*[5] Grunow."

"Yes."

"That's the devil who killed my brother." I felt again the pain of that day, and sobs shook my body.

The Germans waited quietly.

"I'm all right." I wiped my eyes. "I can go on."

Another picture. Rommelmann! He'd been there when Romek was killed.

Another man, tall as the first but thin and balding, introduced himself as a prosecutor.

"Can you give us information about what questions they asked your brother?"

"They wanted to know where some papers were. They thought Romek knew. He kept screaming, 'I don't know about any papers.'"

"Can you tell us anything more about your brother?"

"I never knew where Romek went or what he did. I didn't know he was in the underground."

The first man handed me another photograph from the papers in his hand. "Have you ever seen this man before?"

I looked at the face in the photograph—a youngish man, probably in his early thirties. I didn't know who he was, but I recognized him because of the long scar that ran from the base of one earlobe right down his neck and on beneath the collar of his shirt. Yes, I'd seen him before, more than once. Why were they showing me his picture? It must have something to do with Romek.

"Yes, I've seen this man, but I don't know who he is." My voice trembled as I went on. "I saw him at least two times talking with my brother, standing on the sidewalk on Targowa Street in Tarnów. I recognize the scar."

Dr. von Keudell let out a long breath. "Thank you, Mr. Faber," he said. "You've been very helpful."

"How?"

"You've given us the identification we needed. We appreciate your cooperation."

Suddenly, I realized that the man with the scarred face must be the double agent who had betrayed Romek. My identification of him proved that they had known one another. That must be how I had helped. I hoped that was so.

"What will happen to the man you have in jail?" I asked.

"We appreciate your coming," the prosecutor said, "and we'll compensate you for your expenses and lost wages."

"I'm sorry you had to go through so much," Dr. von Keudell added.

"Sorry?" I asked. "I don't think so. Neither are you sorry for what you did to my family."

He stepped back as though I had struck him. "Mr. Faber, I was in the Wehrmacht.[6] I hated the Gestapo.[7] I took this post as consul so I could show people like you that there were decent Germans, too. If there's anything I can do—"

"No," I interrupted. "I want to be left alone. I'm tired."

I turned and walked from the room.

In the weeks that followed, I called the consulate several times, trying to find out what had happened. The answer was always the same.

"Sorry, but it's top secret. We can't give you any information."

That seemed to be the end of the matter, but it was actually the beginning. Memories began to surface: the fear and suffering, the loss of family, the degradation of concentration-camp existence, the struggle to stay alive and sane. Once more the Germans had invaded my life, brought anxiety and pain, and now destroyed the contentment of my new home in America.

I couldn't keep it inside. It had to come out if I was to have peace. So I began….

General-Konsulat
der Bundesrepublik Deutschland
Consulate General
of the Federal Republic of Germany

Az.: V 5 SR Oppermann u.a.

BOSTON,
MASS., 02116
535 Boylston Street
Fernsprecher: KEnmore 6-4414
Telegrammanschrift: Consugerma Boston
Geschäftsstunden:
Montag — Freitag, 9⁰⁰ – 13³⁰ Uhr
Office Hours:
Monday — Friday, 9 AM – 1 PM

October 17, 1966
CM RRR.

Mr. David Faber
79 Benz Street
Springfield, Massachusetts

Dear Mr. Faber:

I refer to the telephone conversation I had today with Mrs. Faber, and ask for your kind cooperation in the following matter:

The District Court of Bochum, Germany, has requested to contact you with regard to the preliminary investigation against Oppermann and others as well as against Hellmann and others who are suspected of having committed murders during the War near Tarnow/district of Cracow and Wilejka, Western Russia. The District Court of Bochum would be grateful if his judge Dr. Froese, who has already arrived in the United States, could hear you as a witness in this matter on Friday, November 11, 1966 at 10:00 a.m. at the following address:

Holiday Inn
30 Whalley Avenue & Rowe Street
New Haven, Connecticut,

where Dr. Froese and a staff member of this Consulate General will expect you. Mrs. Faber told me that you were too busy on Thursday, November 10th.

I would appreciate your letting me know whether the proposed date is suitable for you. It goes for itself that all costs that you may have in connection with the deposition will be reimbursed to you by this Consulate General.

Very truly yours,

Wilhelm von Keudell
Consul

One of the many requests David Faber received from the German consulate, to provide testimony against Nazi war criminals.

CHAPTER TWO

KATOWICE TO SOSNOWIEC *Running*

I heard the key in the lock. The door opened, and Father came into the apartment.

"Eva! Children!" Father called. "Come! I have something important to tell you."

I got up from the sofa as Mother and my sisters came into the living room.

"What is it, Solomon?" Mother asked, frowning. "Is it Romek?"

The Germans had captured my only brother in the first day of the invasion. He had written a message on a scrap of paper and dropped it from the truck taking him to prison. An elderly woman found it. When she brought the note to our house, she looked us over and was flabbergasted. "My God," she said. "If I knew you were Jews, I would never have brought it!"

We knew only that Romek had been stationed in Tarnów, fighting in the 16th Infantry Regiment of the Polish army and was a prisoner of war, until Father got in touch with Mr. Hoffman, who had been Romek's boss before Romek was called up for military duty. Mr. Hoffman was German and Christian, and could find out things we couldn't.

A few days later, he told us Romek was in a POW camp called Buchenwald,[1] and that we could send small packages of

David Faber's family photo

David Faber at age 13, shortly before the war began.

food and clothing.

"No," Father said. "It isn't about Romek." He pinched his lower lip between his index finger and thumb. "It's about us. The Nazis will be here by tomorrow. We have to get away from the border."

"Oh, no!" Mother covered her mouth with her hand. Then she held both her hands against her breast. "Where can we go?"

"We'll go to Sosnowiec first. Maybe we can stay with the tailor there. We've known him a long time. I bought a horse and wagon this morning. We can take more that way than on the train." He paused. "It still won't be very much."

Mother looked down a moment, and then glanced into Father's eyes. "You know best, Solomon."

He sighed. "We'll take clothes, some bedding, and whatever food we have. And holy things, of course." He paused again, his lips in an upside-down smile. "I can't even take my books."

Suddenly, I realized how bad it was. Father spent hours reading the Talmud[2] and other religious books. The most important things in his life were his family and the synagogue. He would never leave his books unless he had to.

I knew there was no choice. It was harder and harder for Father to get fruit—his business was importing and selling it— and most of his German customers would not buy from him anymore. They wanted nothing to do with Jews. We still could go into grocery stores and butcher shops, but refugees from other towns told us that when the Nazis came that would stop.

My sister Fella sighed and ran a hand through her short, dark hair. She probably was thinking of the friends she would leave behind, especially the young men, I thought. Neither she nor Sabina said anything. Yet I knew they would hate to leave just now. Fella was nineteen; Sabina, seventeen. Kreindel and Laika were older and more serious. I wondered what they were thinking.

"Where will we live?" my youngest sister, Sonia, asked. Her chin trembled, and I thought she might cry.

Father smiled at her. "I know it's hard," he said. He nodded reassuringly. "But God will help us."

I wondered where we would go, how long it would take to

David Faber's family photo

SONIA FABER [taller girl; photo c. 1937], David's sister, murdered by the Nazis in Tarnów, Poland, 1942 (Chapter 13).

Sonia is shown here with a friend on a street in Katowice. Sonia was the youngest of the six sisters, immediately preceding David in birth order. Shortly before she was murdered in her teens, she told David, "I don't even know what it is like to be kissed by a boy, and I'm going to die."

get there. Father probably didn't know because the decision was so sudden.

I supposed I'd just have to wait and see what happened.

"When should we leave, Solomon?" Mother asked.

"As soon as we load the wagon."

I was sure I saw tears in Mother's eyes.

She didn't move for a long moment. Then her mouth became a hard, straight line. She nodded, as if in acceptance.

"You children go pack your clothes," she said. "When you've finished, help Papa with the featherbeds. I'll fix something to eat."

My sisters and I got up and hurried to our rooms. I went inside and gently closed the door. Leaning against it, I looked at my things: two long shelves filled with books, some battered ones I'd had as long as I could remember and newer ones still in their covers. Pictures of the family stood on a chest of drawers. There was a special picture of Romek in his Polish army uniform with medals he had won for shooting and sports. I felt a jolt of fear. Maybe I'd never see him again.

A bedside table held a little radio I'd gotten for my last birthday and a marble bear my eldest sister, Rachel, had sent to me from Paris a couple of years before. I was glad she'd never come home. She was safe in England.

It hurt to leave everything behind, like leaving a lot of me. Then I told myself it didn't matter. I was thirteen years old, not a child anymore. I took socks and underwear from drawers, and shirts and pants from the closet. I picked up my tallis,[3] the prayer shawl my parents had given me at my Bar Mitzvah[4] a few months before. I held it tightly against me, then folded it carefully and laid it on the bed with the clothes.

I pulled a suitcase out from the closet. A cousin had given it to me as a Bar Mitzvah present. I was sure no one thought I'd use it for a trip like this. I thought of that cousin, seven years older than I. He was in the Polish army, too, and I wondered where he was. Maybe in prison with Romek. Maybe killed. Maybe we'd all be killed. Father said God would help us, but I was afraid.

I started to snap shut the suitcase but stopped as I looked at

David Faber's family photo

RACHEL FABER [photo c. 1937], David Faber's sister and eldest sibling, left Poland before the war and lived in England (Chapter 7) until she dies in 1978. After Rachel's death, her husband, Leo Wachtel, gave David her prewar family photos, including this one and all the other prewar family photos included in this book.

hat are his current religious views?

David Faber's family photo

FELLA FABER [photo c. 1937], David's sister, murdered by the Nazis in Tarnów, Poland, 1942 (Chapter 13). Fella is shown here on a street in Katowice. Several years older than David, Fella had begged their father to giver her money and permission to emigrate to Palestine, but he refused, saying he wanted the family to stay together.

The Polish inscription on the back of the photo means "a loving remembrance to my family, Fella."

Romek's picture once more. I picked it up, slipped it under the tallis, and closed the case. I turned then and went out, closing the door behind me.

Fella already sat in the living room, her suitcase on the floor by her feet. She motioned for me to sit next to her on the sofa. When I did, she put her arm around me and pulled me against her.

"We'll be all right, David." She smiled. "We'll find a place."

She was like Mother and rarely seemed upset when bad things happened.

"How will Romek ever find us?" I asked.

Just then, Sonia came in, carrying a suitcase in one hand and wiping her eyes with the other. She dropped her case and sat on the other side of Fella.

"I'm scared," she said. "I'm afraid of what's going to happen."

"I'm scared too," Fella said, "but Papa's right. We can't stay here." She put her other arm around Sonia. "But let's try not to make it harder for him and Mama."

Mother called from the kitchen. "When Papa comes from the wagon, tell him the food is ready."

In a little while, Father came back, shaking his head when he saw the three of us sitting on the sofa.

"It's not the end of the world," he said. "At least we have each other." He went down the hall to his bedroom.

My sisters and I went into the dining room to wait. Sabina came in a few minutes later. She was always the last one to get things done. She wasn't lazy; she just moved slowly. Mother said it was because she was a dreamer.

When everyone sat down, Father said the blessing. Mother served soup and cut thick slices of bread. I took a bite and could hardly swallow. My mouth was dry, and my throat seemed filled up. I looked around the table. My sisters weren't eating, either.

Father buttered his bread and took a bite.

"Eat, children, eat," he said. "We don't know when we'll have another chance."

"I've fixed something to take, but we may not have any dinner tonight," Mother added.

Fella dipped her spoon into the soup and raised it to her lips. In a moment, Sabina, Sonia, Laika, and Kreindel did the same. Then so did I.

Father ate slowly, the way he always did. He never ate very much. Thin, about five feet and six inches tall, he always wore a suit. I thought he was handsome, and I was proud of him. I was proud of Mama, too, though she didn't dress up very often. She was too busy taking care of us and the business to pay a lot of attention to fancy clothes. But she was pretty.

After we ate, the girls went to help Mother pack while Father and I carried the featherbeds to the wagon.

Hans Ronczka, a Nazi who lived in the same building, stood on the sidewalk. When he saw us, he nudged his son, Heinrich, who laughed.

"*Ja!*[5] Run! Run!" the boy shouted. He didn't use the dirty words he always yelled when he saw me alone. Heinrich was taller and heavier than I, and he bullied me every chance he got. Now he pointed at me. "The Führer's[6] coming! You'd better get out, you little *Schwein!*"[7]

"Don't answer," Father told me. "Just go on."

A black mare was hitched to a wagon a few yards down the street. She pulled against the rope tied to a lamppost.

"I think she's scared of the featherbeds," I said.

"Probably," Father answered, "but she'll be all right." We walked to the rear of the wagon. "Help me get these in."

One at a time, we lifted the featherbeds and pushed them inside. I climbed up and smoothed them to make a soft floor. The mare stood quietly now. When I finished, I went up to her and patted her neck. She turned her head to look at me. She was beautiful, with a white star on her forehead.

"Do you know her name, Papa?"

"I forgot to ask. You can name her if you like."

"I'll call her Star. That's a good name, isn't it?"

"Yes, David, a very good name."

I slid my hand down Star's face and over her muzzle. She pressed her head against me. She wants to be friends, I thought. Well, she *is* a friend. She's helping us get away from the Nazis.

The girls brought down the suitcases and the bags. Then Mother came, a basket in each hand.

"That's all, Solomon," she said. "I've got food in this." She nodded toward one basket, then lifted the other. "I wrapped your tallis, the menorah, and the Kiddush cup in the Shabbat[8] tablecloth and put them in this one. I'll hold it in my lap."

"Good," Father said. "We'd better get started. You and Sonia ride. The rest of us will walk."

"How do we get up?" Mother asked.

"There's a step by the front wheel. Here, I'll help you."

The wagon creaked as first Mother and then Sonia climbed up and sat on the hard, wooden seat. Mother straightened her skirt and fixed the shawl on her head.

"We're ready," she said.

Father untied the halter rope and stepped in front of Star. He tugged on the rope, and she began to move the wagon down the street.

I was glad to get away. I'd worried that Ronczka and his son might come back. I looked up at the window of my room and then at Father. Why did the Nazis hate us?

I glanced at the others. Everyone looked straight ahead, except Sonia. Her head was bowed as she sat close to Mother on the wagon seat. She's probably crying, I thought. Then I got mad. Why shouldn't she cry? She was leaving everything, just the like the rest of us. I wished I could stop it all, that I could make things be the way they used to be.

It was early fall, but the sun was hot. I began to sweat, and I noticed that the mare did, too. Where the harness rubbed, white foam stood out against her dark hair. It must be hard to pull such a heavy load. Father took off his coat and tie and handed them up to Mother. That was a new thing. I'd never seen him outside in shirtsleeves.

None of us talked. Nothing we could say would help. I thought of Moses leading his people out of Egypt. We had no Promised Land ahead of us.

In the late morning, Mother asked, "Can we stop? I think the girls should ride for a while. And David, too."

"I'm not tired, Mama," I objected. That wasn't true, but I didn't want her to walk along like a peasant.

"I'll get down," Sonia said. "Let Fella and Sabina ride with you, Mama." She jumped down, and the other two climbed up beside Mother.

"Aaaah," Fella said, "that feels good."

Sabina let out her breath and stretched her legs. She closed her eyes as though she didn't want to see what we were doing.

Father let Star rest for a while, then started again. Kreindel, Laika, and Sonia plodded beside me. Sonia looked down. She turned to me and then looked up at Father leading Star.

"I hate the Germans!" she said, her face splotchy. "I hate them!"

Father kept on walking, sweat running down his face, staining his shirt. He stared straight ahead, and I wondered what he was thinking. He must feel terrible, I thought, knowing he can't take care of us the way he always has. I wanted to tell him I loved him. But I didn't know how to say it.

We came to a small river and stopped. "I'll unhitch the mare and give her a drink," Father said. "She's awfully hot."

"And we can eat lunch," Mother said.

Father released Star and led her to the water. "Not too much," he told her, and pulled her away. After he hitched her back to the wagon, we sat under a tree. Mother handed out bread and pastrami and a bottle of red wine. It was like a picnic, except that no one laughed or teased.

"David can lead the horse for a while, Solomon," Mother said as we loaded up. "You must be very tired."

"Please let me, Papa," I begged. I loved Star as though she had been with us forever.

Father smiled. "All right. It will feel good to sit."

He handed me the rope. Star's black coat wet my hand when I patted her neck.

"Good girl," I told her. "Good girl."

We reached Sosnowiec, twenty-five miles away, just at sunset.

Father was walking again. He stopped Star and stood, holding her halter. His body slumped for a moment, and then he held himself erect.

Mother spoke softly. "We're almost there, Solomon. I hope

the tailor will take us in. It will be cold tonight."

I'm sure he will. But if he can't, someone else will. This is Targowa Street; our people live here."

I got down from the wagon and walked beside Father. Soon he turned the wagon to the left through high, wooden gates that stood open. I knew the building and the big courtyard. Mother had brought me here a few weeks before to have the tailor make a special school coat for me, navy blue with big, gold buttons on the front and three smaller ones on each sleeve. I remembered it well because of the silly thing I had done.

We had come a second time for a fitting. The tailor held out the coat, and I slipped one arm into a sleeve. I put my other arm out, waiting for another sleeve. There was only one!

"I don't like this coat!" I said. "I don't want it!"

The tailor looked angry, until Mother laughed and hugged me.

"Oh, David," she said. "You're a funny boy! It's only half done!"

The tailor laughed then, too, and said, "You don't show a fool a half job!"

My face burned, and I felt foolish.

Father stopped the mare in front of the tailor's door, went up, and knocked. When the door opened, he asked the man if there was room for us to spend the night.

"I'm sorry, my house is full," the tailor said. "My wife's brother and his family came yesterday. I'm sorry."

"Oh, no," Mother said. "Where can we go?"

"I think the Clapers may still have room. They live just next door. I'll go with you to ask."

He stepped outside, went next door, and knocked. A man opened the door. The light from the hall cast a glow like a halo through his bushy hair.

"These are my friends, the Fabers," the tailor said. "They've just come from Katowice and don't have a place to sleep. Do you have room for them?

"Yes, come in. They can sleep in the basement."

"Thank you," Father said, a quiver in his voice. He walked back to the wagon. "Come, Mama, these good people will give us a room for the night."

He helped Mother down from the seat. "You and the girls go in" he told her. "David and I will take care of Star."

"All right, Papa." Mother's voice was heavy with tiredness. Both the man and the woman who now stood beside him smiled and held out their hands to draw Mother through the doorway.

"David, start unloading. I'll unhitch the mare and try to find her some water," Father said.

He loosened the harness while I dragged blankets and pillows from the wagon. The woman I had seen opened the door again.

"Bring them in here," she called. "Your mother and the girls have gone to the basement."

I picked up all my arms could hold, then staggered up the steps and into a hall.

"This way," the woman said, leading me to a door near the front of the building. In the light, I saw a short figure, plump like Mother, with jet-black hair piled on top of her head. I followed her into a big kitchen, with pots and pans hanging from hooks on one wall.

She opened another door.

"Be careful on the steps," she said. "Don't fall." She smiled. "Though you probably wouldn't be hurt with all those pillows."

She laughed and then became serious, almost as if she felt it was wrong to think anything was funny.

Mother stood at the bottom of the stairs.

"Lay them on that table, David. Then go and help Papa."

Father had tied Star to a clothes pole at one side of the courtyard. "Help me with the featherbeds," he said.

Just then, the man of the house came out.

"I'm Isador Claper," he said, handing a bucket to Father. "Here's some water for the horse. I'm sorry there's nothing for her to eat."

Father took the bucket from him and set it in front of Star.

The three of us carried the featherbeds into the house.

"Drop it down the stairs," Father told me. "That's the easiest way."

"When you're settled, come have something to eat," Mrs. Claper said as we came into the kitchen.

"Thank you. I'll tell the others," Father said.

The featherbed was slipping from my fingers, and I was glad to let it slide down the stairs. Father and Mr. Claper did the same with theirs, then Mr. Claper closed the door as Father and I started down to the basement.

"Mrs. Claper asked us to come and eat something," Father told the others.

"Let's fix the beds first," Mother said. "It will only take a few minutes, and then we can go upstairs."

There were no bedsteads, just a table and some battered chairs. We spread the featherbeds on the floor and arranged the blankets and pillows on top.

"David, please go upstairs and tell them we'd just like some tea," Mother said. "We're all falling asleep."

"All right, Mama." I felt hungry but didn't want to eat unless the others did.

When I went into the kitchen, two young men were talking to Mrs. Claper.

"Oh, hello," she said to me. "Are you coming up to eat? I'm sorry I don't know your name."

"My name is David. Thank you, but we're too tired. We would like a pot of tea, though."

"Of course." She filled a kettle with water and set it on the stove. "There, that will be hot in a few minutes."

She nodded toward the others.

"These are my sons, Samuel," she pointed to the older one, "and Moishe. They're students."

She sounded proud as she looked at them.

"Hello, David." Samuel smiled and held out his hand.

"Hello," I said.

His younger brother set down his cup and took my hand.

"Hello," he said, "and welcome."

Samuel spoke again.

"I'm afraid it won't be any better here, though. The Germans are everywhere."

His words sent a shiver down my spine. Father thought it would be better away from the border. Now it seemed it wouldn't be. I didn't feel like talking any more. Instead, I watched Mrs. Claper put tea leaves into a big china pot and pour steaming water over them.

"You can't carry this and six cups, too," she said. "Moishe, help David, please."

"Sure. I'll take the cups."

Sabina and Sonia were asleep by the time I got to the basement. Fella, Laika, and Kreindel were lying down, awake. Mother sat in a rickety chair, her face calm, only her eyes looking worried. Father sat beside her, holding her hand.

"Set the pot on the table, David," she said.

"And here are cups," Moishe said, putting them down next to the teapot. "Good night."

"Good night, and thank you," Mother replied.

She poured the tea and passed the cups to us. First to Father, then to the girls and me. It was strange to see her doing that in a basement instead of in our dining room.

The hot tea made me warm and sleepy. But I was too worried to go to sleep right away. Instead, I asked, "Will we find a place tomorrow, Papa?"

"Mr. Claper doesn't think it is safe here. We'll go further east." He smiled. "But don't worry, we'll find a place. Now finish your tea and go to sleep."

Mother reached out and smoothed my hair.

"Yes, David, rest now. You walked a lot today."

I lay down without undressing, and Papa turned off the bare bulb hanging from the ceiling. In a minute or two, I was asleep.

Sometime later, a low rumbling wakened me. I listened as the noise grew louder. Then I heard Mother and Father murmuring to one another.

"What is it, Papa?" I whispered. "The Nazis? What will they do?"

"Go back to sleep, David. It's the artillery, the big guns. We'll be all right tonight."

I closed my eyes but couldn't go to sleep. I was scared as the noise grew louder, coming closer and closer. I covered my head with my pillow to block it out. Finally, I slept.

CHAPTER THREE

Sosnowiec *Arrests*

Mother woke me the next morning. "David, Mrs. Claper has breakfast for us."

I moved across the featherbed. A blister on one heel rubbed against it, and I tried not to yell. I didn't want Mother to know; she'd fuss about taking care of it. I opened my eyes and saw Father sitting in a chair, staring at the floor. My sisters were up, their clothes straightened and hair brushed.

I sat up, put on my shoes, and smoothed my hair. It stuck up in the back, but I had nothing to put on it.

Father glanced at me. "David's ready," he said. "Let's go up." He smiled and turned toward the stairs.

I felt strange in the big kitchen. The sun shone through a window over the sink, bounced off a shiny pan, and made bright spots on the ceiling. It seemed too normal to be real.

"Good morning," Mrs. Claper greeted us. "There are towels in the bathroom. When you're ready, we'll have breakfast."

"Good morning," Father said, "and thank you."

"Yes, thank you," Mother added.

After a few minutes, we sat around the large, rectangular table where Mr. Claper and his sons were waiting. Dishes of butter and peach preserves were in the center, and Mrs. Claper brought a plate filled with thick slices of bread. She poured coffee for each of us. I held the warm cup in both hands and thought how good it smelled.

I took a piece of bread and buttered it. Mother watched me so I was careful not to take too much of the preserves. I liked the spicy flavor and finished it in a few bites. There was more bread and more preserves, but I didn't want to take them unless Mrs. Claper offered them. She looked at me and smiled.

"Have another piece," she said. "I know how hungry young men are."

I glanced at Mother. She smiled and nodded.

"Thank you," I said. The second piece tasted even better than the first, and I took little bites so it would last. I didn't think there was enough for a third.

"What are you going to do?" Mr. Claper asked Father.

Father hesitated and pinched his lip the way he always did when he was worried.

"I don't know," he said. "I thought we would be safe here, but now I'm not sure. What do you think?"

Mr. Claper nodded. "We heard the guns, too. The Germans will be here today or tomorrow."

Sonia took a loud breath. I looked at her across the table and saw her eyes get big. That usually meant she'd start crying.

The big guns of the night before were silent, but soon we heard rifle fire. Then German words, loud and arrogant.

"Komm her, du Judenschwein! Mach schnell!"

"Come here, you Jew pig! Hurry up!"

We stopped eating, food suspended between plates and mouths. Mother reached out and drew Sonia close. Father laid down the bread he had just buttered and stared at the window.

"They're here," he said quietly.

Sonia began to cry, and Mother held her closer.

Father moved to the window and drew aside one corner of the curtain. For what seemed like a long time, he looked without speaking.

We heard more shouts and rifle shots, now mingled with screams. I got up from the table and walked near the window. I wanted to see what was happening, but I couldn't make myself look. I moved closer to Father.

My voice trembled as I asked, "What are they doing?"

He took my arm and pulled me in front of him.

"Look, David," he said. "You're a man now. See what they do."

I forced myself to look. Then I squeezed my eyes shut and told myself I hadn't seen it. But I had. I looked again. Men in black, Hasidic coats, curls swinging[1] across their faces and arms stretched above their heads, stumbled along the street. German soldiers followed close behind, yelling and cursing. An old man almost fell when a soldier thrust his bayonet into the man's buttocks and withdrew it with a jerk. Another man, much younger, stood on the sidewalk, head bowed, rocking back and forth as he prayed. A soldier struck him on the back of the head with a rifle, knocking off his yarmulke.[2]

"Hurry up, you dirty Jew! Run, damn you, run!"

Across the street, soldiers ran up steps, pounded on doors with rifle butts, and shouted. *"Aufmachen, ihr Judenschweine! Wollt ihr wohl aufmachen!"*

"Open the door, Jew pigs! Will you open!"

More men were yanked outside, then beaten on their heads and shoulders. "Aieee, aieee!" I heard their screams mixed with loud German words.

I began to feel sick. I didn't want to see any more, but I couldn't make myself turn away. I felt tied to the window, unable to move, trembling all over. I looked up at Father and saw tears running down his cheeks. I pushed my face against his chest and sobbed. He dropped the curtain and held me.

In a few minutes, I turned around, lifted the curtain, and peered outside. Men from the apartments on the other side almost filled the street. Soldiers prodded them into rows of five and herded them along, stumbling and bleeding. A young man wearing a green jacket jerked from a soldier's grip.

"Run!" I shouted. "Run!"

A soldier raised his rifle and shot him before he went more than a few steps. He fell and lay on the pavement while the others marched away. It was the first time I saw someone die.

This was Sosnowiec, our place of refuge.

The shooting and yelling went on for hours. My family sat in the living room with the Clapers, waiting. I'd never seen Mother just sit and do nothing. She was always cooking or sewing or doing something for one of us. Now she seemed lost. She'd fold her hands in her lap, then raise them in front of her and rub them together. Now and then, she'd take a deep breath and I'd think she was going to say something. But she didn't, not for a long time.

Finally, she asked Father, "Do you think we should go to the basement? Would it be safer there?"

He took his fingers away from his lip.

"I don't think so. Not unless Mr. Claper wants us to."

"Stay here," Mr. Claper said. "It won't make it any worse."

Samuel, the Clapers' elder son, stood and walked around the room. He stopped in front of his father.

"Why are we just sitting here, waiting?" he demanded. "There must be something we can do. Maybe we could hide in the basement—or go out the back door. Maybe we could get across the street where they've already been. Don't just sit and wait!"

Mr. Claper opened his mouth.

"I'm not—"

Rifle butts pounded against the front door. Samuel dropped into an armchair.

"Now it's too late," he muttered.

"Go into the kitchen," Father told us. "Stay out of sight."

Mother and Mrs. Claper pushed us down the hall while Mr. Claper went to the door. White-faced, he pulled it open and stepped back. Two German soldiers burst in.

"Out, all of you! Out!"

The tall, dark-haired one forced Father, Mr. Claper, and his two sons out the door and down the steps, jabbing at them with his bayonet. The other, younger, blond, pink-faced, peered into the kitchen where the rest of us sat around the big table. He glared at us and spit on the floor. Mother straitened in her chair, folded her hands in her lap, and looked directly at him. After a moment, the young soldier looked away, mumbled something, turned, and went out. He seemed almost ashamed.

No one moved or spoke. We knew that Father and the Clapers would not come home.

CHAPTER FOUR

SOSNOWIEC *Where Are They?*

We stayed in the kitchen for a long time, not saying anything. Every time I heard a noise from the street, I envisioned the man praying and the soldier beating him with a rifle.

Mother bowed her head and covered her eyes with one hand. She looked up, and I saw tears on her face. I'd never seen her cry.

"Mama," I said, "mama." I got up and went to her.

She put out her hand and smoothed my hair. "I'm so worried."

Mrs. Claper clasped her hands together and shook them. Then she got up and stood by Mother's chair.

"Please stay upstairs." Her voice shook as she spoke. "I can't bear being alone." She hesitated, then went on. "There's plenty of room now."

"Of course we will," Mother said. She put her arms around Mrs. Claper, and they held each other for a moment.

Mother and my sisters went downstairs to get a few things. I went into the living room and stood by the window. For a few minutes, I heard nothing. Then came yells in German and shots so close together they sounded like a string of firecrackers. When I tried to reach out to lift the curtain, my arm wouldn't move. It felt cold and stiff. I tried again, harder. Finally, I raised it, pulled aside the curtain, and peeked out.

An old man was on his knees, reaching for his hat on the pavement in front of him. A soldier's boot came down on his hand. The old man's mouth opened, but no sound came out.

I didn't want to see any more. I turned away and sat in a big, leather chair. I could still see the old man's twisted face. Mother and my sisters were in the bedrooms, but I didn't feel like talking. I wandered from room to room. All I could think of was Papa and what the Nazis might do to him.

Mother prepared the beds for that night and sat down at the kitchen table.

"Stay with me," she said, "and you girls, too."

Mrs. Claper sat down with us. I saw tears on Sonia's face.

Mother saw them, too, and held out a handkerchief.

"We have to hope they're all right," Mother said.

"How can we?" Fella demanded. "You've heard what the refugees say."

Mother closed her eyes; her shoulders sagged. "We have to hope," she whispered. "That's all that's left."

No one said anything more. I tried to believe that Father wasn't hurt; instead, I remembered what I saw in the street. But now, it was my Papa I saw stumbling and bleeding, not strangers. My chest hurt until I almost screamed.

Sabina looked up, her head tilted to one side. "Listen," she said. "It's stopped. I don't hear anything."

It took a minute to realize what she meant. Then Mother said, "They must be gone." She signed. "We're all worn out. Let's go to bed."

I kissed Mother and said goodnight to the others. Mrs. Claper had laid out a pair of her younger son's pajamas for me. They were blue with white dots. I held them in my hand, wondering if Moishe was dead. I didn't want to hurt Mrs. Claper's feelings, so I undressed and put them on. They were too big all over. Her son was at least six inches taller than my five feet, and he weighed much more than I did.

I got into bed, pulled up the covers, and tried to go to sleep. But that was impossible. I kept seeing the young man praying and the man in the green jacket trying to run away. And I kept thinking about Father.

I tried lying on my back, on my side, and on my stomach, but nothing helped. After what seemed like hours, I heard Sonia and Fella talking and went to their room across the hall.

I stood at the open door. "I can't sleep," I said.

"Come in," Fella answered. "We can't sleep, either."

I sat on the side of the bed, next to Fella. She took my hand and squeezed it.

"Do you think Papa is… all right?" I asked.

"Surely they wouldn't shoot everyone. I've heard that the Nazis use men to do hard work."

"Papa will get sick and die," I said.

Fella sighed. "Maybe they won't make him work that hard."

I thought she said that to make me feel better. But I didn't because I didn't believe her. The Nazis wouldn't care if Papa got sick and died. I hated them!

A clock in the living room struck three times.

"Try to get some sleep," Fella said.

I went back to my room. I wished Romek were there. The others all had someone with them.

Finally, I went to sleep and dreamed that the Nazis had put Father into a cage. I kept trying to break the lock and let him out. Every time I had the door almost open, a soldier would push me away and put on a new lock.

"Aaagh!" I screamed and woke myself.

Mother hurried into the room, brushing her hair away from her face.

"What is it, David? Are you sick?"

"I had a dream about Papa," I told her. "I don't want to talk about it,"

She sat beside me and stroked my head. "Go back to sleep," she said. "It's almost morning."

She went out, and I lay there, determined to stay awake. The dream was too real.

In the morning, I got up before the others. I didn't hear any noise, and when I looked out the front window, I didn't see anybody on the street. I wondered where Father was. Was he alive? Were the Germans making him work? What if the soldiers came back today and took the rest of us?

I began to shake, harder and harder. My teeth chattered, and I staggered to the sofa.

"David!" Mother called out as she came into the room. "Are you ill?"

I tried to stop shaking. "I was thinking about Papa. I'm all right."

She looked worn out, and I saw new wrinkles in her face. The corners of her mouth moved in a tiny smile.

"Come have breakfast," she said.

Mrs. Claper nodded to me as I came into the kitchen.

"Sit there," she said, and waved her hand toward where Sabina sat.

Sabina scraped her chair on the floor as she moved to make room for me. I sat down and looked at the others. Sonia's eyes were red from crying, and Fella stared at her plate.

Mrs. Claper began the blessing over the bread. Her voice broke. No one looked at her, and after a moment she went on. Mother handed me a steaming cup of coffee, and I took bread from the big plate in the center of the table.

Mrs. Claper suddenly cried out. "Where are they? What have the Nazis done to them?" She clenched her hands and held them to her face.

The rest of us were silent. I didn't want to know. That way, I could tell myself Father was all right.

Late that afternoon, the loud noises began again. I hurried to the window and looked out. Hundreds of men filled the street, with soldiers running alongside.

"What is it?" Fella asked.

"I don't know. Lots of men with shovels and brooms."

"Did you see your father?" Mrs. Claper asked. "Or my men?"

"No. There were too many."

Maybe Father was in that bunch, I thought, or maybe in another bunch somewhere in Sosnowiec. Maybe I could find him. I knew I couldn't tell Mother. She would be afraid. But I couldn't sit and wait.

I walked to the kitchen and back. Mother sat on a wooden chair, clinging to the arms as though she were afraid of falling. Mrs. Claper stood at one side of the room, holding a large, framed photograph of her sons in both hands. She looked at it for a few seconds and then held it against her breast. Fella and Sonia, hands clasped, sat on a sofa with big, blue cushions. I didn't see Sabina, Kreindel, or Laika. They had probably gone to their bedroom.

No one paid attention to me. I listened for noise from the street. Nothing. There was a good chance I could go out without being seen. I went to the kitchen and slipped out the back door.

CHAPTER FIVE

Sosnowiec *Rescue and Murder*

I stopped in front of the building and peeked around the corner. No one was in sight. I had no idea where Father might be, but Sosnowiec was not a huge city. If he was in a work gang, it probably would be on one of the main streets. I could look on all of those.

I started toward the center of town, running from doorway to doorway. A soldier might come around the next corner any minute. He would probably shoot me, but I had to take the chance. It was the only way I might find Father.

Near the end of the fourth block, I crouched in a doorway and caught my breath. It was another warm day, and sweat dampened my shirt. I pulled out a handkerchief and wiped my face.

Suddenly a dog growled. A high-pitched scream followed. I couldn't see anybody from the doorway, so I crept to the corner and slowly put my head around the edge of the building.

Men worked on a side street, sweeping and filling potholes. A soldier stood at the end nearest me, a big German shepherd on a leash at his side. That was what I had heard. But why the scream?

I had to get closer to see if Father was in the gang. It was a long way from the corner to the first doorway. They would see me if I ran. I dropped to my knees and crawled along the sidewalk. By the time I reached the doorway, my knees were skinned, and one palm was cut on a piece of glass.

The dog snarled. I heard shouts in German and another scream. A man lay on the pavement, the dog tearing at his clothes. A soldier jerked the dog away and kicked the man in the side.

"Get up!" he shouted.

The man got on his hands and knees and stayed there for a moment. The soldier hit him across the back with his rifle butt.

"Get up!"

The dog strained against its leash.

I held my breath. Maybe that was Papa! The man struggled to his feet, facing me. No, it wasn't. This man was much younger.

I sighed in relief, and then felt ashamed. Father had taught me

I should feel as bad about things happening to a stranger as I would if it were someone I loved. But I couldn't.

I still didn't know if Father was with these men. The soldiers surely would see me if I moved out of the doorway.

There were more shouts in German. I held my face close to the wall and looked out. The men came to the cross street, and I saw each face as they turned. No, Father wasn't with them.

When they were out of sight, I left my hiding place. Block after block, I ran and hid until I reached the main street of Sosnowiec. A few Polish men were on the sidewalks, and occasionally a car or truck went by. I had to stop running and hiding. I looked straight ahead and acted as though I knew where I was going. A German army truck came toward me, and I wanted to dart into a doorway.

No, I thought, then they'll come after me.

I forced myself to keep walking, afraid to look to see if the truck slowed down. It passed by, and I clung to a lamppost, trembling all over.

By mid-afternoon, almost at the other side of the city, I saw another bunch of men several blocks ahead. I got closer and saw they were digging trenches in the street. That seemed strange.

I came within a block, hiding in each doorway. This work gang was bigger than the first, maybe several hundred men. It would be hard to find Father unless I got much closer.

Three-story apartment houses lined the street. If I could cross over and get onto a roof, maybe I could see if Father was there. But if I crossed at the corner, the soldiers would see me. I decided to turn onto the side street and go along until I was out of their sight.

I got around the corner and raced to the other side. In front of me I saw an open gate behind the corner building. It was probably for deliveries and for carrying out trash. Maybe I could get in the back way. I slipped through the opening and along a narrow walkway to the rear entrance.

Be unlocked, I prayed, and then I grabbed the knob and turned. The door opened. I hurried inside, found the stairway, and went up to the flat roof.

When I thought I was above the men, I dropped to my hands and knees and crawled to the low wall along the front. Slowly, I raised my head and looked over it.

The work gang was directly below me. I looked from one man to another. There was Father, third from the end nearest me! He looked awfully tired, but he was alive.

Father raised a pick over his head and drove it into the ground, again and again. My stomach tightened as I watched and heard the *chunk, chunk*. My joy at finding him turned to fright. I had told Fella the Nazis would kill him that way.

Another man, older than Father, pushed a shovel into the loosened dirt and tossed it to one side. Already the men were knee-deep in the ditch.

I thought of the Clapers and looked for them among the rest of the gang. Was that Mr. Claper, shoveling almost at the other end? The man stopped to wipe his forehead, and I could see his face. Yes, it was Mr. Claper. He looked as worn out as Father.

His sons must be there, too. Then I saw them working close together. Like Father, each of them had a pick.

Father had to get way before the hard labor killed him. But how? Soldiers stood on both sides of the men, their rifle barrels reflecting the late afternoon sun. I watched and noticed they did not pay close attention to the prisoners. Most of the time, they talked with one another. And there weren't too many dogs. Maybe Father could slip away, if he could get around the corner to the side street without being seen.

I picked up a piece of gravel, aimed, and threw it. It landed in the trench in front of Father. He looked up and opened his mouth.

I went rigid with fear. He was going to shout for me to get out of sight! Instead, he raised the pick and struck the dirt. Once more, he lifted it and looked up.

I pointed to the street corner and motioned for him to slip away. He nodded and kept on digging. Soon the soldier closest to him turned and walked toward a guard on the far side. They talked for a while, and one pointed to the workers. Both soldiers laughed and began talking again.

"Now, Papa!" I muttered. "Now!"

As though he heard me, Father slid the pick onto the loose dirt and ran. I held my breath, waiting for shouts and gunshots that never came. He escaped! I looked back at the street and saw the old man shovel dirt over the pick.

I crawled halfway across the roof, and then ran to the corner building. I yanked open the door and pounded down the stairs. Halfway down, I saw Father below me.

"Papa!" I rushed down the steps between us and threw my arms around him. "Papa," I sobbed. "Papa! You got away!"

I pressed against him, his sweat-soaked shirt wet against my face. He held me tightly and ruffled my hair. Then he pushed me away a little.

"Look at you," he smiled. "You're almost as dirty as I am. What would Mama say?"

I tried to laugh but couldn't. He looked so tired and old.

"Oh, Papa!" I said and hugged him again.

We stood there a moment more.

"We've got to get out of here," Father said. "People will hear us. Let's go up on the roof so I can rest."

We started up the stairs, making as little noise as possible. Father went first, breathing hard as he lifted each foot and put it heavily on the next step. He reached for the iron railing and pulled himself along. I wondered if he would make it to the top.

He stopped when we reached the landing on the top floor.

"I have to stop," he gasped. He leaned against the wall and closed his eyes.

"Let me help you, Papa. Take my hand, and I'll pull you."

"In a minute," he said.

I looked at him and grew more and more angry. His hat and tie were gone; his clothes were rumpled and smeared with dirt. He looked like a tramp.

He opened his eyes. "Let's go on."

"I'm all right now," he said. He put his right foot on the first step, grasped the rail, and pulled himself ahead. I stood close behind, ready to push or to keep him from falling. His left foot lifted to the second step, then his right to the third.

He pushed open the door at the top of the stairs, and we went out onto the roof.

"Let's sit down here," he whispered.

I sat close to him, my head against his shoulder. The sun warmed us, and I felt drowsy. I shook myself and looked up at Father. His head rested against the rough boards of the shed and his eyes were closed. His mouth opened. He began to snore, very softly. I didn't want to wake him, so I just sat there. Finally, he stirred and opened his eyes.

"I haven't heard anything, Papa," I told him. "I don't think they're looking for you."

"Let's see what's going on."

We crawled to the front and looked over the wall. Nothing had changed except that the trenches now were as deep as the men's waists. The soldiers didn't seem to know one prisoner had escaped.

I heard the rumble of a motor, then saw an army truck turn the corner a block away. It stopped a few feet behind the prisoners, and an officer got down from the cab. He walked toward the rear, shouting to the ten or twelve soldiers in the truck. They jumped to their feet and pushed against one another, hurrying to follow his orders. Each carried a machine gun.

"What are they doing, Papa?" I whispered.

He didn't answer.

The soldiers ran to one side, lining up along the trench, guns pointed toward the workers.

The officer shouted something I didn't understand, then raised his arm and shouted again.

The noise of machine guns filled my head as man after man fell into the grave he had dug. For an instant, I thought of the shooting gallery at a fair the year before. Then I saw Moishe Claper, whose blue pajamas I had worn the night before. Blood ran down his face. He clutched his stomach, staggered, and fell on top of the dead. I didn't see Mr. Claper or Samuel. Maybe they had already fallen.

"*Sh'ma Yisrael, Adonai Elohaynu, Adonai Echad,*"[1] Father cried out in Hebrew. "Hear, O Israel, the Lord is God, the Lord is One."

He went on, "The Lord is my Shepherd..." Tears streamed

down his face.

I joined in, but my voice failed when we reached the words, "Yea, though I walk through the valley of the shadow of death."

Sobs shook me. I got dizzy and vomited until I gagged. I was a man, I told myself. But this was too terrible. I felt numb and couldn't cry any more.

Father finished the Psalm and peered over the wall again. I forced myself to look. The horror must have been over in a few minutes, but it seemed forever.

The last man had fallen. The guns were quiet. An arm or leg stuck up here and there. At some places, bodies lay half outside the trench. One or two men who must have tried to run away lay sprawled on the pavement. The officer motioned toward them. Soldiers grabbed their legs and dragged them into the trench. They looked down at the bodies for a few minutes, then the officer shouted again. The soldiers climbed into the truck and rode away.

"Let's go," Father said.

We got up slowly, our bodies stiff from lying on the roof. Father stumbled and fell to his knees. He grunted as he pushed himself erect and reached to take my hand. Without speaking, we crossed the roofs and started down.

"Don't make any noise," Father warned.

I nodded and made sure I stepped carefully. On the last flight of stairs, I heard a door on the ground floor open and close. Father tightened his grip on my hand, and we listened. A woman's footsteps came toward the rear of the hall. My heart pounded, and I held my breath.

The footsteps halted almost at the bottom of the stairway. I heard the *whoosh* of trash going down a chute, and let out my breath. The footsteps went back down the hall, a door opened and closed. It was quiet again.

Father smiled at me. I tried to smile back, but my face felt frozen.

"We'll make it, David," he whispered.

We went down the few remaining steps and out onto the sidewalk. Nobody was in sight.

"That's good," Father said. "We'll just have to look out for soldiers."

We walked fast, stopping now and then while Father leaned against a building to rest. The big gates to the courtyard were open when we reached the Clapers' building. We hurried through and stopped at the steps leading up to their door. Father put his hand on my shoulder.

"Just a minute, David," he said. "Let me catch my breath."

We didn't hear anything. Maybe the Nazis had come back and killed everybody. I was anxious to go inside, yet I was afraid. Father seemed to sense my feelings.

"We must go up, David. I'm sure they're all right."

He took his hand from my shoulder and gently pushed me forward. At the top of the steps, he hesitated, then knocked. No answer. He knocked again, harder.

I heard a shuffling sound inside, then saw a window drape move a few inches. Father knocked a third time and called out, "It's Mr. Faber and David."

We heard hurried footsteps, the sound of a bolt drawn back, and the rattle of the knob. The door opened a crack, and a woman's voice asked, "Is it really you?"

"Yes, it's Mr. Faber and David," Father said once more. "Please let us in."

The door swung open just enough for us to slip through before it closed again.

"Thanks be to God," Mrs. Claper murmured. "We thought you were dead."

We hurried along the hall and into the kitchen, where Mother and my sisters sat around the big table.

"Solomon," Mother cried. "Solomon! David!" She rushed to embrace each of us. "You're safe! You're safe!" Mother said over and over, until Father interrupted.

"Not safe, Eva. Just escaped."

Mother said nothing more, but she hugged me so tightly I could scarcely breathe. It made me feel safe, no matter what Father said.

Sabina, Kreindel, and Laika put their arms around both Mother and me, and Sonia and Fella hugged Father. We all cried a little, even though we smiled.

I noticed Mrs. Claper watching from the doorway, her hand

over her mouth. Father saw her, too, and stopped smiling. She held out both hands, palms up.

Her voice trembled as she asked, "Did you see my sons? Did you see my husband?"

"No!" Father quickly answered. "No, I didn't see them. I don't know where they went."

CHAPTER SIX

KATOWICE *No Return*

"Fella should be coming soon."

Mother sounded anxious as she pulled back the curtain and looked out the window. Fella had taken the train back to Katowice early that morning to see if we might be better off in our old apartment.

"It's too early, Eva," Father said.

The rest of us were quiet, but I got more and more worried the longer Fella was gone. It was almost dark now.

Mother sat on the blue velvet sofa, hands folded in her lap. I took her place by the window.

"Is she coming, David?" she asked.

"No, Mama, not yet."

Suddenly, I thought I saw somebody come around the corner. I held my breath and waited until I was sure. Yes, it was Fella! I recognized the way she walked, as though she always knew exactly where she was going. Staring down the street, I shouted, "It's Fella! She's back!"

Everybody crowded around me.

"Let me see," Mother demanded.

I moved to one side, and she pressed her face against the window.

"Yes." She let out a long breath. "Yes, it's Fella."

Mrs. Claper hurried to unlock the door, while the rest of us stood by the window and waved. Fella saw us and waved back. As she started up the steps, we moved to the door.

Mother was the first to hug Fella, holding her close, saying nothing. Then Father put his arms around her. "Fella, Fella," he said. His voice was soft, and I saw tears on his cheeks.

The rest of us hugged her in turn.

"I'm sure you're hungry," Mrs. Claper said. "I'll get some bread and tea." She went off to the kitchen.

Father led Fella to a soft chair. "Is it any better at home?" he asked.

"I didn't have any trouble, and nothing has happened to the

apartment." She paused as if to collect her thoughts. "The neighbors told me it was hard to get food. They're getting along, but everyone's worried."

"Maybe we should go back," Father said.

"You'd better stay inside here, Solomon," Mother said. "They might take you again."

I could see Father didn't like the idea of our going without him. He argued a little, but he finally agreed with Mother.

We had no trouble on the train the next morning. It was good to be home, yet it felt strange. Much of our bedding was in Sosnowiec, and we had to make do without it. We had left the menorah and other holy things there, too.

We needed food, but before Mother went out shopping, Mrs. Goldman from the next apartment came to the door.

She was Mother's best friend. I thought of her as a grandmother because she was older, with snow-white hair and lots of wrinkles. Now she looked even older and very tired.

"It's good to see you again, Eva," she said. "But where's Solomon? Is he all right?"

"Yes," Mother said. "The Germans took him, but he escaped. He's with a friend in Sosnowiec. We were afraid to have him come on the train."

"Ah," Mrs. Goldman sighed. "The world has turned so evil! Just this morning, all the shops put up signs: 'Jews Forbidden.' What's next?" She put her hands to her head.

"We've got to get food," Mother said.

"Maybe Mr. Hoffman can help," Fella said. "He was so good about Romek."

"He might." Mother went to the telephone and called Mr. Hoffman's office.

She told him of our problem and asked if he could help. She nodded once or twice, thanked him, and hung up.

"He said he'd bring some food this afternoon," she told us. "Enough for a few days."

"Thank God for such a friend!" Mrs. Goldman exclaimed.

"Yes," Mother nodded. "We'll share with you, Emma."

"Thank you. It's so good to have you to talk with."

Mr. Hoffman came late that afternoon, his arms filled with packages of food: potatoes and other vegetables, bread, a roasting chicken, tea, and even fruit.

Mother almost cried as she thanked him.

"I hate what's happening," he said. "I'll help while I can, but I don't know how long that will be." He took Mother's hand in his, held it for a moment and then walked away.

The question of food was solved, but we soon learned of another problem. Hans Ronczka began tormenting us when he saw Sonia standing at the window.

"Filthy Jew!" he yelled. "I thought you'd gone. Get out! Get out!"

Sonia hurried away from the window, but Ronczka kept yelling. Then we heard him in the hall. He pounded on our door.

"The Führer will take care of you!" he screamed. "Then we'll have decent neighbors!"

I wanted to yell back, but Mother held a finger to her lips. He yelled some more then went away.

Mother and I were sitting in the living room three days later when someone pounded on our door. A rough voice shouted, "Open up, *Schwein*! I'll clean out this place myself!"

My sisters ran down the hall from their rooms, their eyes wide with fright.

"What is it?" Fella asked.

"It's Ronczka," I said. "He's gone crazy. He wants to kill us."

"Call Mr. Hoffman, Mama. He's the only one who might help," Sonia said in a shaky voice. "He's only a few blocks away."

Mother went to the phone and called.

"This is Eva Faber," she said. She spoke rapidly, shouting over the noise of the pounding. "Ronczka's beating on our door, threatening to kill us. I don't know what to do."

She listened for a moment, then hung up the phone.

"He'll come right away. He said to go to the back of the apartment and wait."

As we went down the hall, we heard gunshots.

"He'll kill us," Sonia whispered. "I know he will."

"The door's solid," Mother said. "He can't break it down very easily. Mr. Hoffman should be here in a few minutes."

Suddenly it was quiet.

"What's he doing?" My voice was unsteady. "Has he left?"

"Maybe he ran out of bullets," Mother answered. She put her hand on my arm. "Stay here."

"Mrs. Faber! It's all right!"

"That's Mr. Hoffman," I said.

Mother let out her breath. She hurried back to the living room, pausing for a moment to look at the bullet holes in the door. Then she opened it.

"Thank God you're here!" she told Mr. Hoffman. "He would have killed us. How -?"

Mr. Hoffman held up a revolver. He looked grim.

"With this. I'd advise you to leave as soon as you can. I'm sorry, but I can't protect you anymore."

"Yes," Mother said. "We'll leave in the morning. We'll go back so Sosnowiec. May God keep you, Mr. Hoffman."

"And you, Mrs. Faber." He turned and left.

"Maybe it's better this way," Mother said. "At least we'll be with Papa."

CHAPTER SEVEN

TARNÓW *Murder and Warning*

"I should have gone myself," Father said when we told him about Ronczka. "You might all have been killed!" He took Mother's hand. "We must decide what to do. Maybe we could stay with your brother in Tarnów."

Mother nodded. "He has plenty of room."

Father pinched his lip, then cleared his throat. "We'll go tomorrow, if we can get tickets."

Fella got up from her chair and walked to the window. She looked out for a minute or two, then turned and took a deep breath. "I'm not going," she said. "It's not safe anywhere in Poland."

"Fella!" Mother said. "We must stay together!"

"I want to," Fella said, "but we've got to get away from the Germans."

"Where do you think we can go?" Father asked.

"Let's go to Lvov. From there we can get into Russia."

"Russia!" Father said. "They won't let us in."

"I'm going to try," Fella said. "The Germans are going to kill us here."

Father tried to persuade Fella to go with us to Tarnów, but she did not change her mind. He went with her to the station the next morning and saw her off on the train to Lvov. Later the same day, the rest of us took a train to Tarnów.

Uncle Hanoh and Aunt Sarah lived in a large, second-floor apartment overlooking the main marketplace in Tarnów. My cousin, Leib, was with them, and so was his fiancée, Helen. Leib was a tall, broad-shouldered man, in his early 20s. Helen was also quite young, and I thought she was very pretty. Their wedding had been postponed because of the war, and she had stayed on instead of trying to go home to Katowice.

The morning after our arrival, we sat around the kitchen table. Father took his fingers away from his lip. "We can't live off you, Hanoh," he said. "We've got to find some way to get food. I'm going out."

"Don't worry, Solomon," Uncle Hanoh interrupted. "Rest a few days and—"

"No," Father said. "I want to do something right away. I'm sure I can do business with the farmers. What food we don't use, I can sell to neighbors or in the market."

Mother looked up. "I'll go with you, Solomon."

"We'll have to walk," he said. "That will be too hard for you."

"I can do it. And besides, I don't want to just sit here all day."

He thought for a moment, then smiled. "All right, Eva."

Except for Shabbat, they went out every morning. Usually, they brought back more than we needed. Everyone had trouble getting food, so it was easy to sell what we didn't eat.

One morning during the second week, they were out buying, and my sisters had gone downstairs to the market. I was on the sofa in the living room, Helen next to me. Uncle Hanoh sat in a big chair by the window, reading. Aunt Sarah stood close by.

Suddenly, we heard heavy footsteps running up the stairs. Before we could do more than look up, something slammed against the door, and it crashed open.

A soldier holding a machine gun stood in the doorway, and I could see others behind him. Helen screamed and threw herself on top of me. The machine gun fired. I felt Helen's body jerk as the bullets hit her. The shooting stopped, and I heard the soldiers go back down the stairs. Then it was quiet.

I lay there, eyes closed, feeling Helen's weight on my back. Finally, I opened my eyes. Uncle Hanoh sagged in the chair. Aunt Sarah lay sprawled on the floor.

I felt cold and began to shake so hard that I was afraid I would push off Helen's body. I didn't want to do that. Aunt Sarah shouldn't be on the floor, either.

Still shaking, I crawled from under Helen and carefully pushed her body against the back of the sofa. Her blood soaked the cushions and smeared on my hands.

I went to Aunt Sarah. She lay on her back, eyes open. It wasn't right for her to be like that. I went to my room, took out my tallis and yarmulke from a drawer, and put them on. I got fresh, white sheets, carried them back to the living room and spread one over each body. Then I clasped my hands in front of me and bowed my head.

"The Lord is my Shepherd, I shall not want...."

I finished the Psalm and sat down in a straight chair to wait for Father and Mother. The next thing I knew, Mother's arms were around me. She held me close, saying nothing as sobs tore my body.

We couldn't stay at Uncle Hanoh's apartment after they were killed. We had to go elsewhere. Father went out to look for another place early the next day and came back a few hours later.

"There's a temporary synagogue over on ulica Szeroka," he told us. "We can move into the women's hall there."

The Germans had forbidden Jewish services and closed all the synagogues. Local Jews were using an empty warehouse as a temporary synagogue, which would now be our new home. We bundled a few things together and moved.

The hall was huge, with one window on the back wall, close to the high ceiling. There was no bathroom, only an outside toilet behind the building. Father found a small, wood-burning stove somewhere, and Mother cooked our scanty meals on that. We slept on potato sacks filled with straw.

My brother, Romek, joined us a few days later. After his release from the POW camp, he looked for us in Katowice. Mrs. Goldman gave him the Clapers' address, and Mrs. Claper told him we had gone to our uncle's home. When he got to Tarnów, Uncle Hanoh's neighbors told him where we had moved.

It was wonderful to have him home again. I loved my sisters, but Romek was my big brother. He always took time to be with me, to talk, to play.

I remembered one day in Katowice when he came home from work.

"Take off my shoes," he teased. "I'm too tired to do it."

"If you pay me twenty-five *groszy*,"[1] I said.

He laughed and ruffled my hair. "You drive a hard bargain."

I took off his shoes, and he paid me. That's how it was between him and me.

The morning after Romek's return, I overheard him talking

Photo by Grzegorz Szczerba

The warehouse and former synagogue in which David Faber stayed with his family still stands at Szeroka 5 (second building from the right) in Tarnów, Poland [May, 2004].

to Father.

"Why did you stay?" His voice was loud, angry. "Why didn't you get out, like Rachel?" He stared at Father. "Rachel was the smart one!"

Rachel, our eldest sister, went to the World's Fair in Paris in 1937 and never returned to Poland. When her tourist visa expired, she went illegally to Milan, Italy, and then to Switzerland. A year later, she met a Jewish refugee from Germany, whose wife and children had been killed while running away from Germany. She went with him to England, pretending to be his wife. Later, she married a Polish Jew named Leon Wachtel, whom she met in England.

Father smiled in his gentle way. "Romek, don't worry. God will help us."

"Yes, God will help us. And they'll kill us all." He paused.

"Why do you think they let me go? Me, a Jew?" He shook his head. "By the rules of war, they couldn't kill me in a POW camp.[2] But here, they can do anything they want."

Father became too ill to go out to the country. But that was the only way we had to get food and a little money.

"I can go by myself," Mother said.

"No, Eva," Father said. "You can't do that. David will go with you."

"Yes, Mama. I'd like to go. There's nothing to do in this place."

"All right," Mother smiled at me. "You're a man, David. You can help."

Mother and I went out every morning except Shabbat, about three or four miles along the road to Dombrowa. We met the farmers on their way to town: old men with sacks on their backs and using walking sticks, old women with long skirts and dark scarves tied over their heads. They carried baskets and sacks filled with vegetables—potatoes, cabbages, tomatoes, carrots, and beets. Some had butter pushed down into big enamel cups and covered with a cabbage leaf, or chickens hanging from long sticks, or baskets of eggs.

Prices were lower out on the road because the farmers did not have to go all the way to the market. Mother could sell what we didn't need for more than she paid for it.

One morning, we met a farmer with eight pigeons.

"I think I'll buy those for supper tonight," Mother said. "We can put them in the box we brought to carry chickens."

I thought the pigeons were beautiful, especially one that was all white except for its head, which was a soft-grey color. It seemed different from the others, too. They just sat in the box, but his one kept moving around and was always turning its head from side to side.

When we got to Szeroka 5, I hurried up the stairs.

"Look, Romek!" I said as soon as I got inside the warehouse. "Look what we got today! Pigeons!"

"I see," he said. "They'll make a good supper."

Mother came through the door. "Yes, we'll eat them tonight."

"Oh, please, Mama," I said. "Don't kill the white one. I want it for a pet."

"What will you do with a pigeon? We don't have any place to put it. And who's going to clean up after it?

"I'll do it, Mama. I promise. Just let me keep it."

"Oh, all right," she said. "But be sure you do, or we'll have to get rid of it."

I ran back downstairs and over to a nearby park, looking for something the pigeon could roost on. I found a log, about four feet long, and dragged it home.

"I can put this in the corner, Mama," I said. "Then Kubush can roost on it. I'll put papers on the floor all around it."

"Kubush! Where did you get that name?"

"I don't know. I just like the way it sounds."

I didn't always pick up the papers right away, and whenever she saw pigeon droppings, Mother scolded me.

"Is this what you want?" she would ask. "This is what I get for letting you keep it."

She scolded me, but she wasn't really angry. She fed it every day with the wheat she toasted to use for coffee.

The pigeon got used to me and would sit on the log while I talked to it, tilting its head form side to side, staring at me first with one eye, then the other.

One morning, two weeks later, someone left the window open, and Kubush flew away. I watched him circle a few times and then fly out of sight.

"Will he come back, Mama?" I asked. "I don't want to lose him."

"I don't know, David. Pigeons like to fly around. It might get sick and die if it stays in the warehouse."

Kubush didn't come back that night or the next day or the next. I thought maybe he had flown back to the farm, or maybe somebody had caught him. I was sure I would never see him again.

Then at breakfast one morning a week later, Kubush flew in through the window and landed on the table in front of me.

"Look, Mama! It's Kubush! He came back!"

The pigeon waddled up to my cup of hot tea and stuck his beak into it. We laughed as he jerked back his beak and shook his head as hard as he could.

"Get him off the table, David," Mother said, "before he does something. I'll get some wheat for him."

Kubush flew back outside, and I followed to see where he was going. As I stepped through the door, I heard the cooing of many birds. A whole row of pigeons sat on the edge of the roof across the courtyard from the warehouse.

"He's brought all his friends, Mama! They're probably hungry, too."

Mother spread the wheat on the floor of the balcony. Kubush began to peck at it, and about a minute later all the pigeons settled on the floor and began to eat. When they finished, they flew away.

They came again the next morning and every day after that for more than a week. They always came at approximately eight o'clock. Mother would say, "It's almost eight o'clock. I'd better get the food ready."

And then we would hear the whirr of wings and the pigeons' feet scratching on the balcony floor. Mother and I would toss the grain to them, then they would eat and fly away.

A skinny, old woman in an apartment across the courtyard yelled at me every day after the pigeons started coming.

"Why are you feeding those dirty birds?" she would scream. "You and your pigeons! They'll bring all kinds of diseases. You're intruders anyway. You don't belong here!"

I thought she looked like a witch, her bent figure covered with a long dress and a scarf that hid most of her face. People in the other apartments laughed at her.

"Don't mind her," they told us. "She's always that way. She's lived here so long she things she owns the whole building."

Then, one morning, the pigeons didn't come. After we had waited fifteen minutes, Mother said to us, "Birds can feel things. There's a reason they didn't come."

"Oh, Mama," Romek said, "I'm sure it's all right. They probably found another place to get food."

"No," Mama said. "There's a reason for everything. I feel danger. Everybody should hide. Please!"

"All right, Mama, we'll hide," Father said. We climbed into

the secret place that Romek had made in the hollow wall between the apartment and the stairwell.

After less than a half hour, we heard heavy boots tramping up the stairs on the other side of the wall, then banging on the doors and guns firing. We heard our door hit against the wall and someone say, "There's nobody here."

After it had been quiet for a long time, we climbed out. Romek and Father went to look in the other apartments.

"Everybody's dead," Father said when they came back.

Mother was right.

CHAPTER EIGHT

Pustkow *The First Camp*

"David," Mother said, "please run down to the corner and buy some milk. There's none for the coffee."

She handed me some money.

"Yes, Mama. And can I get something for myself?"

"Some chocolate, you mean." She smiled. "All right, here's twenty-five *groszy*, but don't eat the candy until after breakfast."

I put on my jacket, picked up the empty milk bottle, and went outside. It was early May of 1940, a beautiful morning. The sun felt warm on my face, and I whistled as I hurried along Szeroka to the little store at the corner of ulica Lwowska.

Nothing bad had happened for a while. Romek was home; that made everything better. Mother was doing well at buying from the farmers. Jews were still able to move about and to buy from neighborhood stores, though they had to wear white armbands with a blue Star of David on them. My family wore the armbands, but I didn't. I thought I could be defiant. People worried about what the Nazis might do, but we got along pretty well.

I was almost at the corner when I heard the engine. I turned as a German army truck jerked to a stop on the other side of the street. A soldier jumped down from the back. Another got out of the cab.

"You!" the first one shouted. "*Komm her!*"

For a moment, I was too scared to move. I felt like the sun had stopped shining. What did they want? I hadn't done anything. I knew that didn't matter. They'd do whatever they wanted.

"Run!" the German yelled, pointing his rifle at me.

I forced myself to run to where they waited.

"Get in!" the soldier yelled and hit his rifle against my back.

My hands slipped as I grabbed the side rail and tried to pull myself onto the high truck bed. I reached up again. Something hard jabbed against my bottom and thrust me across the rough edges of the truck. I scrambled to my feet and saw the soldier climbing in behind me.

He pointed to one of the benches along each side.

"Sit!"

I sat up straight and tried not to let him see how terrified I was as I watched him sit across from me, his rifle on his knees.

The driver got back into the cab, and we started off. As we turned the corner onto ulica Lwowska, I stared at the little store. Ten more feet and I would have been inside!

A little farther on, the truck stopped near four men standing in front of a café. The German guarding me jumped down and shouted.

"*Komm her*!" He pointed his rifle at them, and they walked slowly toward him.

"Get in!" They climbed up, and he motioned for them to sit beside me.

I started to ask the man next to me if he knew what was happening, but the soldier yelled.

"Shut up! Just sit!"

The truck went a few more blocks, turned around, and went back up Lwowska, the main street of Tarnów. Every once in a while, it slowed as though the driver were looking for something.

My hands gripped the edge of the bench so hard they began to hurt. I put them in my lap. They shook, and I pushed them under my legs so no one could see.

There was no chance to get away. The soldier watched us all the time and never put down his rifle. I worried about my family. They'd think I was dead.

It seemed like a couple of hours before we left Tarnów. Soon we turned off the highway onto a narrow road. At about noon, we reached a place where tall pine trees grew close together. The road twisted between them until we came to a clearing where I saw many houses—nice houses, made of wood with brick on the front walls. They had flowers in the yards.

We went on through more forest into another open space almost covered with tree stumps. A high fence was on the far side, and there was a gate with a sign that read "Pustkow[1] Vacation Camp."

A guard swung open the gate, and we drove through. Finally, we came to a big, open space with wooden barracks around the sides. The truck stopped in front of one of them.

"Jump out!" the soldier in the truck yelled at us.

Photos courtesy of Ghetto Fighters' Museum Archive, Israel

These photos [1941] show Jews arrested by the Germans in the Tarnów ghetto, standing on trucks on their way to the Pustkow forced labor camp. On the opposite side of the street stands a group of women and children, apparently the prisoners' families. Three of the people in this group have armbands.

I jumped and stood behind the truck with the others. What was this place? What would happen to me?

A door slammed. I looked and saw a man in civilian clothes coming down the steps, a pencil in one hand and a big tablet in the other.

"You!" he said to the first man. "What's your name?"

The man answered. The German wrote in the tablet and turned to me.

"Name!"

"David Faber," my voice shook as I answered.

"What?"

I swallowed and tried again.

"DAVID FABER!"

He wrote in the tablet and yelled at the next person.

When he had all our names, he motioned for us to follow him into the barrack. Inside, he pointed to a bunk on the lowest of three rows.

"You'll sleep there," he told me.

"Could I be on the top?" I asked.

"Why?"

"I don't know. I just like the top."

He looked at me, then shook his head.

"OK, since you're the littlest one."

"Where am I?" I asked. "Why did they bring me here?"

"You're here to work. Do what you're told, and nothing bad will happen."

We stayed in the barrack the rest of the day, waiting. Nobody knew anything. I lay on the top bunk, scared, wanting to be home. Romek had probably looked for me. Maybe the storekeeper saw the Germans take me away. Even if he told Romek, that wouldn't help. I turned onto my stomach, my face pressed against the straw mattress. I'd never see Mama and the others again. I told myself I was too old to cry, but it wasn't true.

Before daylight the next morning, a loud clang woke me. A man walked up and down the center of the barrack, swinging a big, brass bell. I clamped my hands over my ears to shut out the awful noise.

"Get up!" he shouted. "Get up! *Schweinehunde!*"[2]

With only one thin blanket, I had been too cold to take off my clothes. Mama always wanted us to look nice, so I tried to smooth out the wrinkles. I wondered if she had cried much.

People were lined up in front of a barrel with steam coming from it. A man dipped big, red bowls into it and handed one to each person. As I got nearer, I smelled coffee. The man held out a red bowl, and I took it in both hands. It felt good on my cold fingers. Another man handed out slices of dark bread.

I remembered breakfasts at home, and the bread stuck in my throat.

Suddenly, a loudspeaker boomed out, "*Appell! Appell!* Roll call! Roll call!"

People started to crowd through the door, hurrying into the big, square space between the buildings. The man who wrote down our names the day before stood at one side, holding the tablet. He called out names and put people in work gangs of about thirty. There were at least twenty gangs, each hauled off in trucks.

My crew went to cut down trees. When we got there, the work boss handed me a single-bladed axe.

"Here," he said. "Chop the branches from those trees on the ground. Get them all. I want clean trunks."

I was a city boy. The only times I had been in the country were for picnics. I had never used an axe before and didn't know how to handle one. But I had to do it.

I walked to the nearest fallen tree, lifted the axe, and swung straight down at a large branch. The blade barely cut into the wood. I pulled it out and swung again, striking a spot several inches away. I made cuts in many places, but I didn't seem to be any closer to chopping off the branch.

An older boy working near me laughed. "Hey," he called. "You don't know how. I'll show you."

He stepped over the trunk and came up to me.

"Watch," he said. "First, you hit at an angle this way." He drove his axe into the wood, loosening a large piece. "Then you hit it on the other side, like this." He hit the branch, and the loosened piece broke away. "Try it."

He watched while I swung the axe. It wasn't as easy as it looked, but I kept trying and soon chopped pretty well. Long before noon, though, I had big blisters that broke and stung. When we stopped to eat, my hands were raw, and my whole body hurt.

The man in charge, the *Kapo*,[3] gave us bread and kielbasa. I held the sausage in my hand, wondering if it was pork.[4] Whatever it was, I was too hungry not to eat. I shrugged and took a bite.

The afternoon was worse. My hands bled, and the axe felt heavier each time I lifted it. It didn't cut as well, either, as the blade dulled. By the time we quit work after sundown, it was hard to pull myself into the truck.

Supper was ready when we got to the barrack. No bread, just watery soup in our red bowls. It tasted like potatoes, but it didn't have anything solid in it. The warmth felt good in my stomach, though I was still very hungry. I didn't know which hurt more—my hands, my muscles, or the sharp hunger pangs. Too worn out to think much about it, I climbed up on my bunk and lay down in my clothes again, still wearing my shoes. They were all I had. Someone might steal them if I undressed.

Every day was the same. The bell clanged before daylight; we worked in the forest until dark. The branches scratched my hands and tore my clothes. Each night, I went to sleep hungry and exhausted.

The *Kapo* wasn't mean to us. We could talk to one another, as long as we didn't stop working for more than a few minutes. I tried to make friends with the other boys in the crew, but they were older and seemed not to want me around them.

I did make friends with one of the men. He was in his twenties, five feet six inches tall or so, thin, with brown hair and large, brown eyes. The second day of work, he began talking to me as we chopped on the same tree.

"Where are you from?" he asked.

"Tarnów. But really from Katowice."

"I'm from Tarnów, too. I'm Aaron Weinberg."

"My name's David Faber."

We liked each other right away and tried to work together. After a couple of days, Aaron asked the boy who slept next to me to trade bunks. Then we talked every night about our families and how much we wanted to get out of Pustkow.

Aaron was a tailor who had married a girl named Halka just before the Nazis came. They lived with her mother and father while they saved money for a small apartment.

"I went out to get cigarettes," he said, "and ended up here. Halka doesn't know if I'm dead or alive."

"That's what happened to me when I went for milk. My parents and my sisters and my brother don't know what happened to me."

Aaron was a friendly person, with whom it was easy to get along. He reminded me of Romek, and I looked up to him in much the same way. Neither of us had other friends there.

One night, I asked him, "Do you think there's any chance to escape? I've got to get home."

"There has to be," he said. "I'm not staying here forever. I know this area a little. Halka and I used to have picnics near here on Sundays. I'm getting out, somehow."

"I'll go with you."

He hesitated.

"Please, Aaron."

"OK." He smiled. "We'll try soon."

"What day is it? How long have I been here?"

"It's Friday. You've been here almost three weeks. It's almost the end of May."

Aaron stood next to me in the truck going to work, two days later. "Today," he whispered. "Watch me. Run when I do."

"OK," I said.

I closed my eyes and thought about being home.

We reached the clearing and got off the truck. Aaron and I picked up axes.

"Run the second you see me go," he said.

Just then, another truck drove up, soldiers standing in the back. Three of them got out, rifles slung over their shoulders. The truck turned and went back down the road.

"My God!" Aaron said. "Four guards today instead of just one!"

The soldiers spaced themselves all around the clearing. There was no chance to slip away. Maybe there would never be. It was a terrible letdown. I had worked up my courage, and now it was hopeless.

I worked all afternoon without talking. It hurt too much to think I would never be home again.

Aaron tried to encourage me as we lay on our bunks that night.

"There'll be a chance, David," he said. "Maybe tomorrow or in a few days. There must have been trouble with one of the crews. That must be why they brought in extra guards."

I tried to believe him, but I couldn't.

It was worse the following day. A whole truckload of guards came into the camp before we went out to work, and from then on, we had eight guards with each group. We didn't know why.

Week after week, the guards stayed. We gave up hope.

New prisoners were brought to Pustkow every few days, and they told us the Russians were fighting the Nazis. Pustkow was near the border, and the Germans probably thought we'd try to escape.

Somehow, Aaron kept track of the days, and in early August, things changed once more. We didn't know why, but most of the guards were sent away. There were only two with each work crew.

"Maybe we can try now," I said to Aaron a few nights later.

"Yes," he said, "before the guards come back."

"Tomorrow?" I asked.

"If there's a chance."

We didn't talk any more. I was afraid if we talked about escaping, it wouldn't happen. For a long time, I lay without moving, my body tense. I fell asleep and dreamed that my legs wouldn't work, and the guards laughed at me. I woke, trembling, my clothes damp with sweat.

That's crazy, I told myself. There's nothing wrong with your legs. You can run. You can run fast. And you're going to get out of here.

At noon, two days later, the fat truck driver sat in the cab, eating. The other soldier sat on a stump, enjoying a sandwich wrapped in cellophane. He never touched the bread with bare fingers. He'd unwrap one side and very slowly bite into the sandwich. It seemed he wanted to make it last as long as possible.

He'd eaten a few bites when he laid down the sandwich, reached for his thermos, and poured coffee from it.

Aaron and I were working on a log near the edge of the clearing. He glanced at the two guards eating their lunches.

"Let's go!" he said.

We dropped the axes and ran hard through the forest. Our clothes caught on the bushes, we stumbled over roots and stones, but we kept going until my legs felt like lead and my throat burned.

"I have to rest," I gasped to Aaron, running in front of me.

He stopped and looked back.

"Just a little farther, David. There's a road up ahead. You can make it."

In a few minutes, there it was. A dirt road, full of ruts, with branches hanging over the sides. I stumbled out and collapsed on my stomach, hardly able to breathe.

Aaron sank down beside me, panting.

"Listen, David," he said, one word at a time. "I can't take you with me. "They'll be looking for a man and a boy. If we split up, both of us will have a chance."

I didn't want him to leave. How could I get home by myself?

"Please, Aaron," I began.

He put his hand on my back and shook his head.

"It's better to split up," he said. "Believe me. You go that way." He pointed to the right. "It'll take you farther into the forest. I'm going the other way.

"When the road ends, go on through the forest. You'll come out near a village. There's a farmhouse on this side of it. I know the people. They're good Christians. They'll take you in and give you something to eat. If they can, they'll take you to Tarnów."

He stood up. "Now we've got to go on."

I looked up at him and began to cry.

"Why don't you let me go with you?"

"I can't," he said. "I'm sorry, but I just can't take you."

I knew I couldn't change his mind. I got up and put my arms around him.

"Thank you for everything, Aaron," I said. "Good luck."

He rubbed my head. "Be careful, David. God go with you." He turned and began running down the road.

I did what Aaron said. I didn't know anything else. I went to the end of the road and on into the forest. It was gloomy under the trees, and I was frightened. Each time I heard a noise, I was sure a German was about to grab me.

All of a sudden, I heard a shout.

"Stoy!"

I knew that was Russian. It meant "Stop!" I had heard Mother speak Russian. It was one of several languages she knew.

"Stoy!" The shout came again. *"Ili ya budu streliat'!"*

I didn't know those words, but I guessed he said he'd shoot if I didn't stop.

CHAPTER NINE

Russian Partisans *Sabotage*

I raised my hands above my head.

A giant of a man came toward me, wild looking, with long hair and whiskers all over his face. He pointed a rifle, old and scratched, like something a hunter might have. The only words I understood were "Spy!" and "Come!"

He stepped behind me and pushed the barrel against my back. I started walking straight ahead and hoped that was what he wanted me to do. He didn't say anything, just stayed close behind me, the rifle pointed at my back.

In a few minutes, we came to an open space where I saw four tents. Three of them were the same size, big enough for five or six people.

The fourth was at least three times as big as the others.

"Stoy!" the man shouted when we got in front of the big tent. He called out something, and another tall man came out.

I heard the word "spy," then the second man grabbed my arm and slapped my face, hard.

I rubbed my cheek. He jerked me toward him and slapped me again. It hurt more than anything the Germans had done to me.

A third man, even taller than the others, ducked under the tent opening. He was bald, with a fringe of dark, brown hair covering his ears, and a big moustache curving around his upper lip. A dark-green coat reached halfway to his knees, held at the waist with a very wide brown leather belt. Dark-green pants were tucked into scuffed black boots.

He looked at me and spoke to the men. All I understood was "boy."

I kept saying in Polish, "I don't understand. I don't understand." He didn't answer. I decided to try another language.

"Yiddish," I said.

"Stop!" he told the man who gripped my arm.

"You speak Yiddish?" he asked, in Yiddish.

"Yes."

"You are Jewish?"

"Yes. I just escaped from a work camp, from Pustkow."

"I know that place. How did you get away?"

"I ran when the guards weren't looking. I'm not a spy. I want to go home to my family. They don't know what happened to me." I felt tears in my eyes.

He smiled, and the corners of his eyes wrinkled.

"My name is Sasha," he said. "Don't worry. You're with the partisans.[1] You're safe here."

He spoke Russian to the others. I supposed he was telling them about me. All the time he kept his hand on my head.

He turned back and spoke to me in Yiddish.

"You'll have to stay with us. You can help fight the Germans." He motioned for me to follow him into the tent.

"You must be hungry," he said. An enormous round loaf of dark bread lay on a crude table made from small branches crisscrossed over one another and nailed together. He picked up a knife and cut a big hunk from the loaf.

"Pokushai!" he said. "Eat!"

That bread tasted better than any cake I had ever eaten!

"We need all the help we can get," he said when I had finished.

"I'll do anything. Just tell me."

"Later," he said. "Rest now."

I lay down on the canvas floor, pulled a thick grey blanket over myself and closed my eyes. It was hard to believe that I was safe, that I would have enough to eat and a warm place to sleep. Maybe if I did what Sasha wanted, he would let me go home before long.

Someone shook me. I opened my eyes and saw an old man bending over me, his long grey beard brushing against my face.

"What do you want?" I asked in Yiddish. "Who are you?"

The old man's eyes almost closed as he smiled, and he said something I didn't understand. He motioned for me to get up.

"Nemnozhki pokushai, malenkii," he said and pulled on my hand. "Eat a little bit, little one."

I got up and followed him outside. It was almost dark, but I could see boys and old men sitting and standing around a campfire.

"Pokushai," the old man said again.

Sasha turned from the fire.

"Here," he said in Yiddish. He held out an enamel cup filled with hot soup, thick with potatoes. As I sipped, the old man watched and smiled.

"Good," he said. "Good."

"That's Uncle Vanya, our cook," Sasha said.

I sat on a small log near the fire and finished eating the soup. With my stomach full, it was hard to stay awake.

Sasha laughed. "Go to bed, David," he said. "Tomorrow I'll show you how to help."

Early the next morning, I wakened to Sasha's booming voice. "Get up, get up!"

I opened my eyes and saw him standing over me like a giant.

"Come, eat," he said. "Then I'll take you with me."

I threw off the warm blanket and hurried outside. Uncle Vanya put wood on the fire beneath a soot-covered coffeepot.

"Good morning!" he shouted.

"Good morning!" I answered, as I went off into the woods.

By the time I had come back and washed my face and hands, Uncle Vanya had poured coffee into my cup. He handed it to me and pointed to chunks of bread piled in an enamel bowl.

Sasha came from the tent as I was eating.

"Finish, and we'll go," he said. "It's getting late."

I swallowed the hot coffee as fast as I could. I'd finish the bread on the way.

Sasha started off through the trees, and I hurried behind him. He took big steps, and I had to run now and then to catch up with him. The corn on a little toe burned as my broken shoe rubbed against it.

After an hour or so, Sasha stopped and looked back at me limping along. He shook his head, took a blanket from his rucksack, and spread it on the ground.

"Lie down, *malenkii*, and rest."

I lay down, and he covered me with the blanket. It seemed as though I'd just closed my eyes when I felt his hand on my shoulder.

"Let's go," he said. "It's not far now."

I got to my feet, Sasha stuffed the blanket into his pack, and we walked until we came to a break in the trees.

"There." Sasha pointed to a bank about twenty feet high. "The railroad tracks run on top." He pulled a long knife from a scabbard on his belt, bent down, and began to dig near the bottom of the slope. I wondered what he was trying to find. In a couple of minutes, he uncovered a long crowbar and a wrench. He picked them up, and I followed him up the embankment.

"Watch," he said. "See how I'm loosening these nuts that hold the rails on the ties." He knelt down and used the wrench. "I won't take them off. Just make them loose enough to be easy for you to take off." He turned each nut a few times.

"When I tell you, you'll come here and take them off so you can move the rail to one side a little bit. You have to do it at the exact time I say. I'll give you a watch."

He reached into a front pocket and brought out a tarnished watch fastened to a short chain. "Don't lose it," he said. "Your life depends on it."

He went on. "A lot of trains come along here. The one we want comes every day at three o'clock. It's loaded with guns and ammunition. Five minutes before, two men go along on a handcar, checking to see that the tracks are all right. As soon as they're out of sight, you run up here and loosen the rails. You can turn the nuts with your fingers.

"Then pull out the bolts and move the rails with this." He held up the crowbar. "Remember, move the rail just a little bit, about an inch. Then climb a tree and hide until you're sure nobody saw you. They could follow you back to camp."

I didn't want Sasha to see how scared I was.

"OK," I said. "I can do it."

He put his arm around my shoulders.

"You're a good boy," he said. Then he laughed. "Wait until you see what happens to the train."

He put the tools back in the ground, smoothed the dirt over them, and covered it with a few leaves.

I was scared, but I felt proud, too. I'd do something to hurt the Germans. That was good. Even my toe didn't hurt as much walking back to the tents.

I didn't sleep very much that night. Once I dreamed that a German soldier climbed the tree after me. I kept going higher and higher. He was right below me, grabbing at my feet. His fingers touched my shoe, and I woke up, screaming.

Shasha leaned over me. "It's all right, *malenkii*," he murmured and put his hand on my shoulder. "You're safe here."

I shivered and pulled the blanket tight around me.

After breakfast the next morning, Uncle Vanya picked up a pail and motioned for me to go with him. We walked through the pine woods a little way, stopped, and began picking blueberries from a clump of bushes. I helped him pick the big berries, every once in a while putting one into my mouth instead of the pail. They were sweet and full of juice.

Uncle Vanya seemed not to notice at first, but after a while he pointed to my hands and my mouth. My fingers were stained, and my mouth must have been, too. He touched my lip and showed me a blue fingertip. I thought he was angry with me. Instead, he began to laugh, hugged me, and kissed my cheek.

"Good boy," he said.

I laughed, and we picked blueberries until we had filled the pail.

Early in the afternoon, Sasha called to me.

"David, it's time to get ready. Come."

I followed him into the big tent. He went to one side of it and began taking things out of a big box. I couldn't believe it when he held up girls' clothing.

"Wear these," he said. "People won't think about a little girl doing anything."

I didn't like it, but I had no choice. I took the white blouse and dark-blue skirt he handed me, undressed, and put them on.

"Wear this sweater, too," he said. It was a dark-blue with different-colored wool stars scattered over it. I put it on and buttoned it down the front.

I felt silly and was sure I didn't look like a girl.

"Now," Sasha said. "One more thing."

He took out a wig and set it on my head. The long strands of reddish hair fell to my shoulders, tickled my ears, and hung over my eyes. I hated it.

"Now you look like a girl. Try to act like one if you see anybody."

I'll try to act like my sisters, I thought.

"I'll go partway with you," Sasha said. "Then you'll be on your own. Remember what I told you yesterday." He picked up a rifle.

"Take this, too. Hide it if you see anybody." He paused. When he spoke again, his voice sounded harsh, like the man who had brought me to the camp.

"I trust you," he said. "But if you don't do the job right, we'll catch up with you. If you get caught and talk, we'll kill you if the Germans don't. Do exactly what I told you. You'll be OK, and we'll take care of you."

"I'll do it right," I said. "I know I can." I tried to sound brave, but my voice trembled a little.

Sasha squeezed my shoulder. "Yes," he said, "you can."

The pocket watch read 2:27 when I got to the edge of the forest and climbed a tree. At 2:33, a short train rattled by, pulling freight cars.

I began to sweat as it got closer to the time the handcar should come along. Maybe I couldn't move the rail. Maybe someone was watching and would grab me when I was on the tracks. They'd try to make me tell about the partisans, and Sasha had told me what would happen if I did.

2:55. The handcar came down the track. The handles went up and down as two men pushed on them in turn. At the same time, each one looked at one of the rails. I started to climb down the tree, to be ready to run to the track as soon as they were out of sight.

The rails went gradually down a slope, then up again and over a small hill. I scratched my bare legs on rough bark as I half-climbed, half-slid to the ground, ran to the embankment, and dug out the crowbar. I scrambled up to the rails.

The bolts came out just as Sasha told me they would. I stuck the crowbar into the ground and pushed hard. The rail didn't move. Sasha said it would be easy. Maybe for one of the men, I thought. I stepped to the other side of the crowbar and jerked.

Gradually, the rail moved outward. Then I moved the other one in the same way.

I slid down the bank and hid the crowbar. I heard a train whistle in the distance. I had to get back to the trees. I ran to the nearest one, grabbed a limb just above my head, and climbed to the top. Panting, I huddled against the trunk, trying to make myself small. I didn't think anybody saw me.

Now I could hear the engine getting louder and louder. It sounded like it was going fast. My heart pounded against my chest.

The train came into sight, a black monster roaring toward me. Smoke poured from the smokestack; wisps of steam hung alongside. It got closer, and I saw flatcars loaded with trucks and tanks. Soldiers holding rifles stood on each car.

The iron bar moving the engine wheels jerked back and forth, and I held my breath as it roared up to the place where I had shifted the rails. It came so fast I was afraid it would run right across the break. But Sasha said it would wreck the train. It had to work!

Suddenly, the engine jerked toward me, hung for a moment, then toppled over and slid down the bank. It looked like a huge, upside-down beetle, the iron bar still turning the wheels.

Some flatcars followed it, the tanks breaking loose and crashing against the trees. Some of the soldiers jumped free, but I heard one scream as a tank crushed him. For a moment, I felt sick. Then I remembered Sosnowiec. I felt good about hurting the Nazis.

A man crawled out the window of the cab, his face smeared with blood.

Soldiers ran from the back end of the train, carrying rifles and machine guns. One of them pointed toward the trees and shouted. He ran into the woods, and the others followed him.

I pressed against the trunk, trying to make myself even smaller. If they found me, they'd kill me. Or, worse, they'd make me tell about the partisans. Then they'd kill me.

I heard the Germans yell at one another for a while, then the sounds faded as they went back to the train. Some of them climbed onto the cars still on the tracks; others went back toward the caboose. They must have thought whoever wrecked the train had gotten away.

When it was too dark to see the soldiers on the flatcars, I climbed down and ran toward the camp. My foot caught on something, and I fell, scratching my face on a bush. I lay flat, panting.

"David! David!"

I knew that voice. Sasha! I'd be all right!

I got up. "Mr. Sasha! I'm over here! I did it!"

He came up to me and grabbed me in a bear hug. "You did a good job," he said. "Let's get back to camp."

The others sat around the fire as we walked into camp. Sasha pushed me in front of him.

"This boy did it!" he shouted in his deep voice. "He did it!"

They all jumped up and crowded around me, laughing, talking, trying to hug me. Each one told me what a great thing I had done.

I looked at them, boys no older than I, and old men, and I felt proud.

Uncle Vanya came last. He hugged me and kissed my cheek. *"Tovarishch!"* he said. "Comrade!" He hugged me again.

As the days went by, I wondered how the partisans got food. There seemed to be plenty, but I never saw anybody bring it. Somebody must be helping them. No one told me anything, and I was afraid to ask questions.

For me, the camp was almost like a holiday. Uncle Vanya and I became good friends. He would slip extra pieces of kielbasa or cubes of sugar into my pocket. Every morning, I would go with him to pick blueberries or hunt for mushrooms. He would hang the mushrooms on a string until they dried, then slice them and put them in the potato soup.

The next three weeks, Sasha and I went to different places along the railroad. He'd loosen the nuts, and I'd come back the next day and move the rails. We didn't always walk. Once, we rode in a wagon for almost five hours. I didn't know where it came from. Like the food, it was just there waiting on the dirt road.

Each time, I felt good when I saw the cars tumble off the tracks and knew I had hurt the Germans a little bit.

After supper one night in early November, Sasha brought an accordion from the tent. He sat on the big, flat stone that held down a tent rope and began to play. The party went on for hours, the others singing and dancing to Russian folk music. Even Uncle

Vanya danced.

Finally, Sasha stopped.

"David," he said, "*Tovarishch*. You'd better go to sleep now. You have a big job tomorrow."

I knew what he meant. We had gone again that day to get things ready.

The next day, I put on the girls' clothing, and Sasha arranged the wig. The long hair bothered me as it always did, and I pushed it off my face.

Sasha jerked away my hand. "Don't do that!" he roared at me. "I've fixed it just right. If you move it, your own hair shows. Leave it alone!"

I had never seen him so angry.

"I won't touch it," I said. "I won't."

That day, I went to a place not far from the first wreck. I dug out the tools and started up the embankment. Then I saw them! Far off, soldiers walking toward me. One of them pointed and yelled something I couldn't hear.

I dropped the tools and ran back into the forest. Soon I smelled something. I stopped and sniffed. Smoke! I heard faint crackling sounds. The woods were on fire! The Germans must have done it!

I had to do something, quick.

I remembered a story about a boy who was caught in a fire when he was hunting in the forest. He covered himself with dirt and breathed through a gun barrel.

I looked around. The trees were far apart, and there were spots with almost no needles. Maybe it would work. I dug in a bare place with my rifle barrel, scraped out the dirt with my hands, and dug again. I dug and scraped as fast as I could until the hole was deep enough.

I hit the rifle against a tree and broke off the barrel. Dirt clogged one end, and I poked it out with a stick.

The noise of the fire was much louder now, and smoke burned my eyes. I took off my sweater, lay down on my back, and pulled dirt over myself. I put the sweater over my eyes and held the barrel to my mouth with one hand. With the other, I piled dirt around the barrel and over my face. I breathed as little as I could, afraid the smoke would strangle me. I was afraid, too, the ground would get too hot. But it was my only chance.

If I died, Mama and Papa would never know what had happened. Nobody would. Maybe an animal would dig up my body. I had never seen anything bigger than rabbits in the woods, but there might be dogs.

A little smoke came down the barrel, burning my throat. I stopped breathing for as long as I could, then drew in a short breath. It tasted smoky. I tried again. The air was warm, but I could breathe.

The rifle barrel felt warm against my lips. If it got hotter, I couldn't use it.

The Germans were to blame. If they had left us alone, I would be with the family in Katowice. We would be happy like we were before. I wished I had wrecked more trains.

Suddenly, I realized that the barrel was cooler. The fire must have gone past me. I uncovered my eyes and looked up.

A strong wind shook the treetops and blew trails of smoke across them. But the trees weren't burned. How could that be?

I let the rifle barrel fall to one side, pushed away the dirt, and got up. Not far away, smoke curled up from the ground, and everything was black. But the trees around me weren't touched. The wind had made the fire leap past. That's why I was alive.

I had started running sometime after three o'clock. It must be hours later. I took out my watch. 4:22! The fire had gone by in less than an hour, pushed by the strong wind.

I was afraid to walk through the burned woods in the dark. I'd stay where I was until morning, huddled out of the wind against a tree trunk.

A little way off, a fallen branch burned. I'd be warm there.

Ashes crunched under my feet as I walked to it. I sat down and held my hands near the flames. I didn't care how dirty I got. I wanted to be warm.

My eyelids drooped, and I struggled to stay awake, afraid of falling into the fire or the wind blowing sparks onto my clothes. But no matter how hard I tried, I couldn't stay awake. I woke just before sunrise. Shivering, I rubbed my eyes and smelled the soot on my hands. They were black, and my face must have been, too.

I got up, brushed ashes off my clothes, and started to walk. Nothing looked familiar. I wasn't sure which way to go.

I went to the spot where I had buried myself. I came here from *that* side, I thought, so the camp must be in the other direction. I started off again, feeling hungry and very thirsty.

There were no sounds, no birds, no small animals, no rustling needles. My feet kicked up ashes without making a noise. Here and there, smoke curled form a smoldering stump or fallen branch.

Everything was burned, and I got more and more worried about my friends. The camp was deep inside the forest, and they wouldn't have had time to get away. The Germans must have been watching, anyway.

Just after daybreak, I reached the campsite. I found no tents, no ropes between the trees—just bodies, some lying face down, some curled on their sides. The clothes were burned off. The bodies were black. No one who was there could have lived.

I went from body to body, trying to see who they were. I identified most of them, saying the name as I looked at the body. Ivan, the one who had found me and brought me to the camp. Pavel, a boy younger than I. Little Vanya, another boy.

Not everyone was there. A few must have been away when the camp burned.

Sasha was there, his big body lying face-up, most of the wide belt still around him. And Uncle Vanya, curled up at the foot of a tree trunk. I wanted to thank him for being so good to me. I had never done that. I loved Uncle Vanya as though he were my own father, and suddenly I felt very alone. For a moment, I wanted to lie down next to him and be dead too.

I didn't cry as I looked at them. Instead, I felt hatred for the Germans. They had started it all.

Suddenly, I became aware of a noise. A plane was very near. I dropped face down. The plane roared overhead. A few minutes after it passed, I started to get up.

I heard it again, coming from the same direction. This time, it seemed even lower, almost on top of me. They must have been looking for survivors.

The plane came again two or three minutes later. I was lying on my side, and as it flew over me, I saw the swastika painted on it.

I waited, but it didn't come back. I got up, said goodbye, and started toward the road I had come down a few weeks before.

The road turned away from the burned area, across a field to the edge of another forest. I walked along, tears running down my cheeks, wondering how I could survive. Just before the road curved around some trees, I heard the creaking of wagon wheels.

I hid behind a tree and waited. A horse came around the corner, pulling a wagon. An old farmer sat in front, his head bowed, his face half-hidden. The horse looked old, too, and it walked very slowly.

As the wagon passed, I ran out behind it. The bed was too high for me to see what it carried. I reached over the tailgate and felt with one hand. Potatoes, covered with straw.

I pulled myself up and into the wagon, hoping the old man wouldn't hear me. He looked almost asleep, and so old that he might be a little deaf. Slowly, I cleared away some straw and made a hiding place among the potatoes. I curled up in it and pulled the straw back over me.

We rode for quite a while, then stopped. I felt the wagon sway as the farmer climbed down. I moved aside some of the straw and peeked over the sideboards. We had stopped at the back of a house, and I watched the farmer go inside. I slipped out from my hiding place and dropped to the ground on the side away from the house.

My hands, my face, and my clothes were black with soot. I was afraid to let anyone see me.

I hurried away from the farmhouse, not knowing what to do. The road crossed another field, and in the middle of the open space I heard a car coming behind me. There wasn't any place to hide before it stopped alongside me.

A young woman was alone in the small car. Her dark hair hung to her shoulders around a long, thin face. She looked at me, then said in Polish, "Don't be afraid, boy."

But I was afraid, too afraid to move or say anything. How did she know I was a boy? I still had on girls' clothing. The wig was gone, maybe that's how she knew.

"You look terrible," she said. "Were you in that fire?"

I was too tired to run anymore. Maybe she would help me. She seemed to want to help. "Yes," I said.

"You must be one of them. Did anybody else get away?"

I knew what she meant. I didn't answer, just shook my head.

"You're so young," she said. "Come, get in the car."

She opened the door, and I got in.

"Here, lie down on the floor, and I'll put this blanket over you."

She took a plaid car robe from the back seat. Maybe she was playing a trick and would turn me in to the Germans.

"Why do you want to help me?" I asked.

"Don't ask questions. I'll take you wherever you want to go. Now lie down."

I had to trust her. There was no one else.

"I want to go home," I said. "To Tarnów."

"Tarnów!" She frowned. "Do you know how far that is?"

"No."

"More than sixty miles. It'll take a long time." She frowned again. "Well, I'll take you. But first, we'll stop at the river up ahead, and you can wash. I'll try to get some clothes for you later."

We drove off and soon came to a small stream, where she stopped.

"All right," she said. "You can wash up here."

I got out, took off my clothes, and washed myself. The water was cold, but the sun felt good on my bare skin. I hadn't had a bath in a long time, and it felt good to be clean. The filthy clothes got me dirty again when I put them back on. But my face was clean, and my hands.

She didn't say anything when I got back into the car, just smiled and drove on. Pretty soon, we came to a small town, and she stopped again.

"I'll buy a shirt and pants for you," she said. "Stay covered up."

I wondered again why she was doing all this. Or was she going inside to telephone the Germans? I would have to take the chance.

After a few minutes, she came back. "I got your clothes," she said. "You can change when we get to a place where no one will see you."

I didn't understand why she would risk her own life to help a Jewish boy she didn't even know.

"Why are you so good to me?" I asked.

"Don't ask questions. Leave it to me."

Then she asked, "Why were you with the partisans? I know you're Jewish, not Russian. What did you do with them?"

I told her about running away from Pustkow, but I didn't tell about wrecking the trains.

"Would you tell me your name?" I asked.

"Lola. And yours?"

"David Faber."

She stopped again. "You can get out here and change clothes behind those trees. Hurry, before anyone comes by."

It was good to get rid of my clothes, as much because they were girls' as because they were filthy.

When I got back to the car, I started getting cramps from being squeezed between the seat and the engine.

"Can I get up on the seat?" I asked.

If you keep your head down and the blanket over you," she said.

We went through another town, and I peeked over the edge of the door. *Rymanów Hat Works* I read on a building.

Soon we came to Jaslo, and I knew I was nearly home.

We got to Tarnów just at sunset. Lola sopped on ulica Walowa, four blocks from home.

"Won't you come and meet my family?" I asked. "They'll be so grateful. Maybe you'd like to stay overnight. It's a long way back."

"It's better if we aren't seen together," she said. "I know Tarnów very well, and I have friends here. I can stay with them."

I held out my hand. "Thank you very much," I said. "Whoever you are, God bless you!"

She shook my hand but said nothing. I stood at the curb and watched until she turned the corner a block away.

I couldn't believe there was someone like that, who would risk her life to save mine. But I didn't even know if Lola was really her name.

I ran the four blocks to Szeroka 5. A few months earlier, it was just a place to stay. Now it was home. It was hard to wait after I knocked. My youngest sister, Sonia, opened the door. Her face was blank for a moment, then she began to shout.

"Mama! Mama! David's home!"

She put her arms around me and began to cry.

I stepped inside as Mama ran to the door. She hugged me to her, then put her hands against my face.

"So thin," she said. "Come, I'll get you some food."

Everybody crowded around, crying, hugging me.

"We thought you were dead," Papa kept saying.

Mama gave me bread and milk, and I thought of the milk I hadn't bought.

They wanted to know everything.

"Not everything tonight," Mama said. "David looks worn out. He should go to bed soon."

I was too excited to sleep. I told them about being picked up, about Pustkow, about the Russians. When I told about wrecking the trains, Romek smiled at me.

"I'm very proud of my brother," he said.

That was almost the best thing about coming home.

CHAPTER TEN

Tarnów *Passes and More Murders*

Early one afternoon about two weeks later, Romek came into the room, closing the door slowly behind him. He stood there without saying anything.

"What is it, Romek?" Father said, looking up. "Did something happen?"

"There are signs all over. Jews have to register at Gestapo headquarters. Anyone who doesn't register will be shot."

"When?" Father asked.

"In three days. But I think we should go right away."

Romek took me aside. "David," he said, "when we get there and the Gestapo asks your name, report like a soldier. Stand up straight and tell them that you're eighteen and a metalworker. You'll probably be safe if they think you can do work like that."

I was sure they wouldn't believe me. I was only fourteen and small. But I trusted Romek.

Mother seemed more worried than the rest of us. "David," she said later that day, "I'm going to fix something that may help you if the Germans pick you up again."

"What, Mama?"

"I'm going to bake bread and hide my gold wedding chain in it. I'll make a little bag for it, too."

She made bread, cut a kind of lid on the top, and picked out the soft part. She folded the long chain Father had given her and stuffed it into the hollow loaf. Then she pushed the top down over it.

"Put this in the bag," she said. "Take it whenever you go out. Someday you may be able to use the chain to buy things." She sighed and hugged me. "But promise me that you'll eat the bread if you are starving. Promise, David."

"I promise, Mama."

The next day we went to register. Sonia held a handkerchief to her mouth, and her eyes were shiny with tears. I looked at her and took her hand. I grew more frightened the nearer we got to Gestapo headquarters. My sisters looked scared, too. We moved closer to

David Faber's family photo

EVA FABER [photo c. 1937], David Faber's mother, murdered at about age 54 by the Nazis in Tarnów, Poland, 1942 (Chapter 13).

Eva is wearing the gold wedding necklace described in Chapters 10 and 14.

Eva Faber was born to a wealthy family in Berlin, Germany, around 1888. She fell in love with Samuel (Solomon) Schwarc, a poor Yeshiva student from Poland, whom she married against her father's wishes in a Jewish religious ceremony in Poland. When the couple went to register their marriage at the Polish town hall, Solomon was attached by a group of hoodlums who set his beard on fire. (Beard-burning attacks on Jews are also reported in Daniel Goldhagen's *Hitler's Willing Executioners*, p. 189). Much of his face got burned, and he refused to have his picture taken thereafter. Solomon and Eva escaped, but Solomon never returned to the town hall to register the marriage or to change the name of his wife to Schwarc. Eva Faber retained her maiden name, and all eight of their children, of whom David is the youngest, were named Faber.

Father and Mother walking a few feet ahead.

Romek put his hand on my shoulder. "Remember what I told you," he said.

A flag hung from the building at the next corner. I could see the black swastika as it moved in the wind. A line of people huddled against the grey, stone wall and reached almost halfway down the block. I wanted to turn and run in the other direction, but I knew I couldn't.

We took our places behind the last person in the line, Father in front and Romek in back. I felt cold, partly from the wind and partly from being afraid. Every few minutes the line moved ahead, and soon we were at the entrance.

Father turned to us. "Trust in God," he said. Then he led us up the steps, past the soldier guarding the door, and into a big lobby. I saw a huge picture of Hitler on the wall, a swastika on each side. Below it, Gestapo officers sat behind a row of desks.

We waited our turn. The only sounds were of shoes shuffling on the marble floor, the harsh voice of the Gestapo man asking questions, and the softer response of the person standing before him.

Slowly we moved forward. I watched the persons ahead of us as they walked the last few steps. I thought how different they seemed. A few old men and women seemed proud, but most looked scared. As I got closer to the front, my terror grew. I'd try to do what Romek had told me, but I didn't know if I could. I didn't know if I could talk at all.

I watched Father, then Mother and my sisters, stand before the desks. I was afraid Sonia would cry, but she didn't.

It was my turn. I hesitated, then pulled back my shoulders and took three steps forward. The young, blond man behind the desk glanced up at me.

"*Ich melde. Herr Oberstführer, ich bin achtzehn Jahre alt,*" I said. "I report to you, colonel, sir. I am eighteen years old."

The Gestapo officer stared at me. I was sure he knew I was lying. I looked fifteen or sixteen, at most. After a long moment, he stamped a paper and held it out to me. I looked down and saw the black image of the German eagle.

Romek was the last to register. In a strong voice, he reported his age and skills.

Father and the rest stood on the sidewalk, waiting for Romek and me to come out. Without saying anything, we started home, holding our passes in our hands, walking fast. Once or twice, Sonia or Sabina said something but no one answered. I felt as though we had come to the end of one life and the beginning of another.

We showed one another our papers when we got home. My sisters' passes were stamped with a *K*, and so was Father's. Mother's and Romek's had an eagle with a swastika under it, like mine.

Romek frowned. "One must be worse than the other."

He stood for several minutes, chin cupped in his hand. Then he looked at Father.

"I think the *K* passes mean they'll pick you up, maybe for a labor camp," he said. "You've got to hide somewhere."

Romek was university educated, spoke several languages, and was trained as a metal engineer. He always seemed to know what to do. He looked around the room. "There's a lot of space back under the attic stairs," he said. "I'm going to cut a hole in the wall. All of you with *K* passes can hide in there."

He went to the basement and came back with a saw. Then he cut out part of the wall close to the floor, about three and one-half feet wide and about two feet high.

"Come help me, David," he said. I went with him to the basement and got knotty pine boards we had seen there earlier. Leaving the hole open, he nailed the boards onto the wall. Finally, he made a cover for the hole.

"All right," he said. "You girls crawl in. You, too, Father. I'm sure there's enough room."

"Will they be all right?" Mother asked. Is there enough air?"

"Yes," Romek said. "It's the only place they can hide." He put on the cover and laid a straw sack against it.

Mother sat on a straight chair Father had brought home a few days before. Romek and I sat on the straw sacks. Romek looked at Mama. She looked tired, worn out from all of these troubles. She was getting old fast, and you could see on her face that she was getting sick. She was fifty-two years old.

Romek said, "We have to do something about your being older. Old people they kill, and young people they take for forced labor. So, Mother, we have to put some makeup on your face and make you look young, and dress you young, so that when they come in and they look at you they won't see you as an old woman but as a young lady."

He was writing and figuring something out. In about half an hour, he came to me and said, "I have it! I have an idea."

He made some kind of paste, a face cream, out of a mixture of vegetables, juice from carrots, parsley leaves, a finely ground potato, boric-acid water,[1] and other ingredients I can't remember. He smoothed the paste over Mama's face. She kept it on for about three hours. After she washed it off, her wrinkles had disappeared. Her face was so pretty, I couldn't believe it. My brother went on, dressing my mother like a young lady and fixing her hairdo like a young lady's which made her look very beautiful.

Then Romek said, "Now what we have to do is be ready for them."

It was hard to stay awake as we waited to see if the Germans would come. We talked a little about good times in the past, and tried not to think about what was happening.

After an hour or so, we heard rifle shots. Then there were heavy footsteps in the other part of the synagogue.

"Quick!" Romek said. "We don't want them looking around."

He opened the door between the rooms and motioned to us.

"Hold your pass so they can see it. Don't make them ask for it."

Two soldiers shouted at us as we stepped through the door. "Stop!"

They looked surprised to see us, holding out our passes. Romek was a soldier and had been a German prisoner of war. He knew the German ways of doing things. He stamped his shoes together and saluted the Germans with two fingers to his head like a soldier. At the same time that he showed them his pass, he introduced Mama by her first name. "This is Eva, and this is my brother, David." The smaller soldier stared at Mother – he seemed to be admiring her – while the other one looked at our papers.

"Get back!" the second one said, his voice harsh. We turned and hurried inside. Romek closed the door, and we heard the soldiers tramp back toward the street.

"What did they want, Romek?" Mother asked.

"I think they were looking for *K* passes."

"Thank God you hid Papa and the girls!"

I was wide-awake now, and scared. I could hear noises from the street: shooting, shouting, screaming. I wondered why they had left us alone. Romek was probably right. They were taking people with *K* passes. They'd put them someplace like Pustkow or maybe kill them.

The commotion went on and on. Romek looked worried. He kept getting up and walking around the room. Finally he said, "Mama, you'd better hide, too. I'm afraid they'll come back."

He took the cover off the hiding place.

"Are you all right, Papa?" he asked.

"Yes," Papa answered. "But we were worried when we heard somebody."

"Germans," Romek said. "I think they were looking for *K* passes. I'm worried they'll be back, so Mama is going to hide with you."

I heard scratching and bumping as they made room for Mother.

It was a good thing she hid. Soldiers came again just at daybreak. Romek and I showed them the eagle stamps, but this time it made no difference. One of them, tall and heavy, pointed his rifle at Romek.

"Out, Jew! You can use that pass to get into hell!"

The other one grabbed my arm and yanked me through the door. My feet slipped, and I fell. When Romek helped me up, my legs shook so I could hardly stand.

"What will they do?" I asked.

"Just do what I tell you."

I saw no one on the street. Maybe the other Jews were already taken away. The soldiers marched behind us toward ulica Zydowska, Jews' Street. The taller one said something and left.

I heard rifle shots again. Romek bent down and whispered, "They're shooting in the market. We've got to get away. Be ready."

He took a big, old-fashioned iron door-key from his pocket and held it against his chest. The soldier turned his head, and Romek hit his temple with the key. The man dropped and Romek pulled him into a doorway.

My brother grabbed my hand and pulled me back along ulica Szeroka. Apartment houses and stores lined the street. There was no place to hide. All we could do was crouch in a doorway.

Romek put his arm around me and held me tight. My whole body shook. I knew the soldier wasn't dead. He'd get help and look for us as soon as he came to. I tried not to cry; I didn't want Romek to be ashamed. But it was hard.

Heavy boots sounded on the sidewalk, and voices shouted in German, "They can't be far away!"

"Will they shoot us?" I clung to Romek as he sheltered me with his arm.

"I don't know, David. But don't let them see you cry."

I wiped my eyes and tried to force back the sobs. They found us in a few minutes, the same two of them. The taller soldier slammed the butt of his rifle against Romek's head.

"Get up, you bastard!" he yelled.

They pushed us into Jews' Street, an alley leading to the market. Three-story houses seemed to lean toward each other, shutting out most of the light. The noise from the market became louder, echoing in the narrow passageway.

More soldiers and prisoners crowded in front of us, filling the alley. Each was wearing a white armband with a blue Star of David on it.[2] The soldiers shouted and prodded, the prisoners stumbled and wailed, calling on God to save them, reciting passages from the Torah.[3]

Suddenly, Romek yanked on my arm and pulled me into a doorway. A miracle! The door was unlocked, and we slipped inside without being seen.

"Up to the roof," he whispered.

We ran up three flights of stairs, and stepped past a large, tin-covered door into what looked like an attic. We heard heavy boots pounding on the stairs below us. We stood behind the door, panting. I heard my brother praying under his breath. Any minute, I thought, the Nazis will look past the door and see us. But they never did. After a while, we didn't hear any more footsteps, and we went up one more flight of stairs, to the roof.

"Lie down," Romek said.

We lay there for a few moments, then crawled to the edge. I looked down into the circle of the marketplace, filled with people. As I watched, soldiers lifted machine guns and fired. Bodies fell on top of others already shot.

I closed my eyes, remembering Sosnowiec. It couldn't be happening again. But it was, only worse. Hundreds were shot there. Now thousands were being killed here. When bodies covered most of the circle, the living were forced to pile them into wagons that hauled them away. Then more were shot.

"I can't watch it, Romek. I can't!"

Romek cradled me in his arms and rocked back and forth.

"Cry," he said, "no one can see you now. Cry!"

Romek's tears spilled down and mingled into mine.

When dark came, we went one floor down, and knocked on a door. A man opened the door. I saw a couple children behind him. My brother did the talking, and we stayed with this family for less than one hour.

A Jewish policeman came over. I thought the policeman would give us away to the Nazis. We said we wanted to go home to see if our family is safe.

"Let's go," he said. "I'll make believe that I'm taking you to Nazis, but I'll take you to family."

We went back out onto Zhedovska and around the corner back to Sheroka. And then he left, and we were with our family again.

CHAPTER ELEVEN

Tarnów *Where's Papa?*

Jews were ordered into a poor section of Tarnów, into a ghetto, just like the old days[1] I'd heard about. We moved from the synagogue to two rooms on the top floor of a run-down building.

A bunk bed was against one wall of the back room. Romek and I slept in the top bed, Sonia and Sabina in the bottom one. On the other side of the room, Laika and Krcindel shared a cot. Mother fixed a straw pallet along another wall for Father and herself.

The kitchen had no stove.

"I don't know how I can cook," Mother said. "We have to get some kind of stove."

"If I can't find one," Romek said, "I'll try to fix something." He went out to look into empty apartments.

We had a square, tin breadbox with a lid, a little more than a foot long on each side and about eight inches deep. Mother had brought it along every time we moved.

"I can make a stove, Mama," I said. "I'll use the breadbox."

With a nail, I poked holes in the bottom and in the lid, so air could pass through.

"Look, Mama. If we make a little fire in here, the top will get real hot."

"But it will burn the floor, David."

"We can set it on a couple of the tiles lying in the attic. That should be all right."

Mother wasn't sure it would work, but when we burned wood scraps in it, it got very hot.

"Such a smart boy, David!" Mother hugged me. "It works fine."

A baker and his family lived in the basement of our building. The room by the entrance held a huge brick oven; the rooms beyond it were their living quarters. Mother had sent me there for bread when we lived in the synagogue, and we bought flour and eggs from him after we moved into the ghetto.

She mixed eggs and water into the flour and fried a kind of bread, which we ate with potato soup. For Passover, she was able to buy matzos[2] from him.

The ghetto quickly became a slum, hemmed in by barbed wire. People crowded into old apartments, usually with plumbing that didn't work and without electricity. The only places to buy food were little stores that had only what was left from earlier days. People began to die, some in their rooms, some on the streets. Every day, wagons carried the bodies to a common pit.

Work gangs went out of the ghetto every morning. I worked on the streets. Romek did, too, when he was home. Sonia, Sabina, Laika, and Kreindel worked in a garment factory. Our only pay was a bowl of watery soup for lunch. We used Mother's jewelry and whatever else we could find in the ghetto to trade with Polish civilians for potatoes and other vegetables. Whatever we got, we hid in our clothes and took home.

The Germans stopped rounding up people and killing them in the marketplace. Instead, soldiers broke into the apartments and shot whomever they found.

Romek decided to fix hiding places as he had done in the synagogue. "Up here on the fourth floor," he said, "we can hear them coming. We'll have time to hide."

Like the synagogue, the apartment had a very high ceiling and stairs that led to an attic. Romek cut a hole in the kitchen wall, this time behind an unframed picture painted on a linen cloth. It showed a mother teaching her children to cook. I wondered about the family who had lived there.

The hole was too high to get into without help. An old chair and a tall wardrobe were left in the apartment, and we used these as steps to get to the hiding place. The only window overlooked a gently sloping roof covered with red tiles. Another roof slanted steeply down to it from the taller building next door. Romek loosened tiles on that roof to make a hiding place. When the tiles were pulled back into place from underneath, it looked as though they had never been moved.

A few days later, he told us he had to leave for a while.

"I can't tell you where I'm going," he said, "but I'll be back soon. I promise."

We worried about him until he came home two weeks later,

thin and worn. I didn't know how he managed to get out of the ghetto and back again. He said nothing, and no one asked.

Soon after, he left again, this time for several weeks. We knew nothing about where he went or what he did. When he came back, Sonia asked where he had been. "Never ask me that question," Romek answered. "If anyone asks, tell them you don't know me, you've never heard of me. You might get tortured and questioned if I tell you anything. Never ask me again."

One afternoon, we heard shots from below us.

"They're coming!" Father said. "Quick! Get under the roof!"

We hurried into the bedroom. Father helped Mother through the window, then waited while the girls and I followed. Mother had moved the loose tiles by the time all of us were outside. Quickly, we crawled into the space between the roof and the attic floor, and Father carefully slid the tiles back into place.

We huddled together, hardly breathing, afraid the soldiers would hear us. Heavy boots tramped through our two rooms, men called to one another, then the sounds died away.

"I'm afraid they might still be looking around," Father whispered. "We'd better stay here awhile."

When we didn't hear anything for a long time, we took off our shoes and slowly moved toward the center of the attic, where there was room to sit or stand. Then we waited.

After a few hours, we heard noises that sounded like shots and like people running.

"It doesn't sound good. I think we should stay here until tomorrow" Father said.

"I'm hungry," Sabine whined. "Can't we get some bread?"

"Listen to Papa," Mother said. "I'm sure he's right."

Sabina sighed and lay down on the dusty floor, her head in Mother's lap.

For the next two days, we heard the soldiers come and go. We talked in whispers and moved as little as possible. The pain in my stomach got sharper and then dulled again. Sabina didn't complain anymore. She slept most of the time, and the rest of us tried to do that, too.

We heard nothing the third day, and when it got dark, I said to

Father, "Let me sneak out to get water and something to eat. We're starving. Maybe I can get something from the baker."

"All right, David. Be very careful."

He moved the tiles enough for me to slip through. I sat and slid to the lower roof, then walked down it to the bedroom window. I didn't hear a sound as I dropped to the floor, then went into the kitchen and out onto the stairs.

Then I kept close to the building as I hurried to the baker's apartment at the end of the hall, next to the street. I went down the cement steps to his door, which I could see was ajar. I pushed it open and stepped into the dark.

My foot bumped something on the floor that didn't move. I knelt and ran my hand over clothes. My fingers touched hair, and I smoothed a short, pointed beard. The baker. All of them must be dead: his wife, his daughter, his two sons.

I stepped over the body and went ahead, holding a hand out in front of me. That rough surface had to be the brick oven. The storeroom was to the right. I turned and walked to it.

Sacks of flour were on the shelf, too heavy for me to carry back across the roof. I felt in the dark, found a bowl, and dipped it into the flour. That's all I could take now.

I turned and started back, then tripped and fell, spilling the flour. I lay across the wife's plump body. Hurriedly, I got up. I had to get more flour. I went back to the storeroom and felt along the shelves until I found a half-filled sack. I could carry that. I slung it over my shoulder and started once again toward the door, sliding my feet for each step, so that I wouldn't fall again.

My hands felt sticky. Outside in the moonlight, I saw they were smeared with something dark. Blood. My clothes were bloody, too, from falling on the woman. My feet were dusty with flour and made tracks on the pavement. I couldn't leave those for the Germans to follow.

I set the flour sack at the foot of the stairs to our apartment and went back outside. With my hands, I brushed away the tracks. Then I went inside, picked up the sack, and climbed to the fourth floor.

I managed to get through the window with the sack and across to the hiding place. I tapped on the tiles and called softly, "Father! It's me. I'm back."

"Thank God," I heard him say. Then he took away the tiles, and I handed him the sack.

Mother sat nearby. "David," she said, "can you bring some water and the tin stove? Then I can make pancakes."

"All right, Mama," I said, and went back into the apartment.

I made two trips, one with a bottle of water and one with matches and the little stove filled with coal.

We stayed hidden for another four or five days, living on the fried pancakes. The first ones were only flour and water, but I went back to the baker's apartment and found eggs. They made the pancakes delicious.

It was now the fall of 1942. One night, all of us were sitting around the table Romek and I had carried home from an empty apartment downstairs. Suddenly, we heard footsteps on the stairs that came three flights straight up from the street.

"It's the Germans!" Romek said. "Quick! Hide!"

Sonia was the first to step on the chair, climb onto the wardrobe, and scramble through the hole. The other girls were right behind, then Mother and I. Romek hurried in after us and pulled the picture into place.

We heard a crash, then the sound of footsteps and a rough voice. "Nobody here!"

"They're hiding! Look, the window's open." This one sounded younger.

"They're under the roof like the ones we found yesterday."

We held our breath and listened to them climb out the window. Their boots scraped on the tiles.

Mother gripped Romek's arm. "Where's Papa?" she whispered. "Why didn't he hide with us?"

Romek groaned. "There wasn't time, Mama," he said. "He hid under the roof."

"Oh, my God! They'll kill him!" Mother's voice shook.

We heard tiles breaking and sliding.

"Here's one!" More words we couldn't understand. The thud of blows. A scream.

We heard the Germans jump down from the window as they came back into the room.

"We got one, anyhow." It was the younger voice.

"*Ja!* Hiding like a rat!" the rough voice laughed. "Come on."

In the dark behind the wall, I reached for Mother. We clung to each other, crying without a sound.

The soldiers tramped across the floor and down the stairs.

"Go look for Papa, Romek," Mother whispered.

"We'd better wait a few minutes to be sure they've gone."

We heard a thump, then slow footsteps. Someone was in the room. Maybe it's a trick, I thought. Maybe one of the soldiers stayed behind. But why would he make noise?

A creak. Someone opened the wardrobe door. Slow steps again. Quiet.

We waited for what seemed like hours, afraid to talk or move.

Finally, Romek whispered, "I think they're gone. We've got to see about Papa."

I slipped past him, out onto the wardrobe. In the candlelight, I saw a white form on Father's straw sack. Without saying anything, I jumped down to the floor. Blood lay on the bare boards in a path from the window to the wardrobe. I followed it to the sack.

Father lay there. Blood oozed from cuts on his head, staining his tallis. Moor blood showed through the white cloth he had put on like a Kittel.[3] His hands were folded across his chest.

I stared, frozen, for a moment. Then I cried out, "Romek! Mama!"

They came quickly. Mother knelt by the bed, crying in great sobs. She picked up Father's hands and held them against her lips.

The Germans had beaten Father and cut him with axes, but somehow he had managed to get inside, get his prayer shawl and the white garment from the wardrobe, put them on, and lie down.

Romek lifted Mother to her feet.

"Mama, Mama," he said softly. He held her, and when her sobs stopped, he murmured, "He died with dignity, Mama. Not in the street."

CHAPTER TWELVE

Tarnów *Is Your Name Romek Faber?*

Three days after Father was slaughtered Romek shook me before dawn as I lay on the straw pallet beside him.

"I'm afraid the Germans will take you the next time they come through," he whispered. "Come with me."

I sat up and rubbed my eyes in the dark. "Where?"

"It's better if you don't know. Then you can't tell."

I struggled to my feet and got dressed. Romek filled a bag with clothes and slung it over his shoulder.

"Come on," he said and started for the door.

I pulled on his arm, and he turned to look at me.

"Mama won't know where I am. We ought to tell her good-bye."

He shook his head. "It's better if she doesn't know. I've left a note."

In the old days, nothing would have made me happier than going with Romek. It would have been an adventure. Now everything was changed. But I trusted him.

I followed him into the summer morning, where we joined a gang going to work outside the ghetto. Soldiers with rifles guarded us. I recognized the Gestapo officer who strutted around, looking at each person. He came into the ghetto often. Everyone knew his name: Grunow.

Romek held my hand. "Don't move. When we're through the gate, do exactly what I tell you."

Grunow said something to a guard, who unlocked the gate and pushed it open. The officer looked at Romek, turned, and went to his car.

We were near the middle of the group, walking in a double column. No soldier was near us as we passed the gate and went on a few steps. Suddenly, Romek grabbed my arm. He pulled me out of the line and through a doorway.

"Go up and hide," he whispered. "I'll be back."

I ran up the stairs, pulled open a door, and went into an attic. My feet made tracks in the dust as I walked to a far corner and sat down. I wondered why Romek had left me there and when he'd come back. Every time I heard a noise I was sure the Nazis were coming. It seemed like hours before I heard footsteps just outside the attic door. It sounded like more than one person. It must be soldiers this time, I thought. I huddled against the wall, closed my eyes, and held my breath as the door opened.

"David?"

It was Romek's voice.

"It's me, Romek, I'm here."

I pushed myself to my feet and rushed to the door.

An older man stood beside Romek.

"This is Mr. Valah," Romek said.

Mr. Valah put out his hand.

"Hello, David," he said. "We've come to get you."

"Hello, Mr. Valah."

I wondered who he was and why he was with Romek. We followed Mr. Valah to an expensive-looking car parked by the curb.

"Get in," he said.

We went several blocks, until we reached ulica Kilinskiego, a street where rich people lived in big houses. Mr. Valah turned in at number 25 and drove to the rear.

"You'll be safe here," he said.

He got out of the car and led us inside. A woman, plump, grey-haired, wearing a dark-blue dress, met us in the hallway,

"This is Mrs. Valah. She'll take care of you."

"Come, I'll show you where you'll be staying." Mrs. Valah smiled. "So you're Romek's brother. You look like a nice, young man."

The four of us went to the basement. Mr. Valah pressed something, and a door swung open in what seemed to be a blank wall. I looked into a large room, furnished with beds, tables, chairs, a radio, and shelves filled with books. One thing was missing. There were no windows. And there was only one entrance.

"You should be comfortable here," he said. "Mrs. Valah will bring your food. She'll give three double knocks on the wall. If there is any other knock, or if someone calls, don't answer."

The Valahs went out and closed the door. I looked at my brother.

"Who are they? Why did we come here?"

He laughed and hugged me. "It's all right, David. We're safe here. I can't tell you any more."

I looked at my watch. Almost eight o'clock. So much had happened in the last couple of hours.

At about nine, we heard three double knocks. Romek opened the door, and the Valahs came in.

"We'll have breakfast for you soon," the woman said. "I'm sure you're hungry."

I hadn't thought about it before. Too much had been happening. Now I realized how empty my stomach felt.

Mr. Valah spoke to Romek. "We need to talk with you."

"Stay here, David," Romek said. "I'll be back soon."

I turned on the radio but switched it off again when there was only talk in German. I read the titles of the books on the shelves, pulled out a novel, and began to read.

I had finished only a few pages before Romek and Mrs. Valah returned with breakfast: thick slices of bread, butter and jam, a slab of cheese, and a pot of coffee. I hadn't seen food like that for months. My stomach growled.

"Don't eat too fast, David," Romek smiled at me. "You'll get a stomachache."

"But it's so good, and I'm so hungry!"

I was ashamed as soon as I said that. He must be hungry, too, but he ate slowly. I put down the bread covered with butter and jam and chewed on the mouthful I already had.

"What did you talk about?" I asked.

Romek shook his head. "If you don't know, you can't get into trouble. Just do exactly what they ask."

Mr. Valah knocked on the door the next morning.

"Here's breakfast," he said. "Eat. Then we'll go."

I wondered where we were going, but I knew I shouldn't ask. We cleaned our plates, then went out to the car.

We were going slowly down a main street when two uniformed Gestapo stepped out in front of us. They held up their hands for Mr. Valah to stop. One came to Mr. Valah's window, the other to the passenger side. Each held a revolver.

A blond man with pink cheeks leaned down and looked inside the car.

"Where are you going with these *Schweinen*?" he demanded.

"Back to the ghetto. They've been working at my house. Is something wrong?"

"And who are you?"

Mr. Valah took out his wallet. "I'm Judge Valah. Here's my identification."

The man looked at it, then handed it back.

"You're lucky you weren't killed!" he said.

"Get out," the other Gestapo shouted at Romek. He was blond, too, and taller than the first man. "Both! Out!"

I was terrified. These were Gestapo. I knew they'd do anything they wanted. I got out as fast as I could and stood by my brother.

"Over there!" The taller man pointed toward an open car parked at the curb. "In back!"

He got into the front seat, facing us all the time, pointing his revolver at us. I could almost feel the bullets tearing through my stomach. I tried to move closer to my brother, but the man motioned with his gun for me to stay away.

After a few minutes, we stopped in front of Gestapo headquarters.

"Get out!"

I tried to follow Romek out of the car, but my body wouldn't move. I sat there, paralyzed, until he took my hand and pulled. Then I stumbled out and stood beside him.

One of the Gestapo prodded Romek with his revolver.

"Inside! Upstairs! Run!"

Inside! I had been inside before when we registered. This was different. Now we were prisoners. I knew we would never get out, never see Mama again.

Romek pushed me in front of him and kept his hand on my back as we ran up the stairs and into a large room. I recognized the man seated at the desk—*Hauptsturmführer* Grunow, the man who had been in the ghetto that morning. Another man was there, too. Rommelmann.

Everybody knew them. They were always in the ghetto

Photo courtesy of Yad Vashem.

A photo of a young German man, thought to be Gestapo officer Otto Grunow of Tarnow, Poland.

Gestapo officer Wilhelm Rommelmann.

whenever anything bad happened.[1]

A wide door that reached almost to the ceiling opened behind Grunow and Rommelmann. Two soldiers carrying machine guns came in and stood, one on each side of the room.

"Sit down!" Grunow ordered.

He stared at Romek. "You! Is your name Romek Faber?"

"Yes."

"And yours?"

"David Faber." I barely forced out the words.

"So you're brothers?" He paused. "I'm going to ask some questions. Every time I hear a wrong answer, you'll wish I hadn't."

Grunow got up, walked to Romek, and stood glaring down at him.

"Where are the blue papers?" he asked softly, almost a croon.

"I don't know what you're talking about. The only paper I have is the *Juden* passport."

"I'm asking about the papers *I* want. You know what they are. I want the blue file, the plans you stole!"

"I don't know about any plans."

Grunow struck him in the face with the back of his gloved hand. Romek's head banged against the wooden chair.

"Again, where are they?" Grunow's voice was louder.

"I don't know."

Grunow hit him again. Blood spurted from Romek's nose.

"Once more! Where are the plans?"

"I don't know about any plans."

Grunow walked to the fireplace at the end of the room. He picked up a poker and stuck it into the red-hot coals that filled the grate. He held it there until the end glowed. Then he came back to stand in front of my brother.

"This is the last time I'm asking you. Where are those plans?"

"I don't know about any plans."

Grunow stared at him. Then he pressed his lips into a tight line, lifted the poker, and jabbed it into Romek's eye.

"Eeeeeeeeee!" Romek screamed. He put both hands to the bloody eye.

"No, no-o-o-o!" I tried to jump from my chair.

A soldier jammed his machine gun into my stomach.

"Stay there or you'll be next!"

"I don't know! I don't know!" Romek kept on screaming. "My God! Oh, my God, let me die! Please let me die!"

"Tell me! Where are the plans?"

Grunow bent over, his face close to Romek's.

"I . . . don't . . . know."

Two more men came into the room and took hold of Romek.

One pushed some kind of metal clamp onto his face and squeezed. It squashed his chin and forced open his mouth.

"If you don't tell where those plans are, I'm going to cut out your tongue." The second man spoke quietly, matter-of-factly.

"I don't know! I don't know!"

The corners of Romek's mouth were torn and bleeding from being opened so wide. Somehow he continued to scream.

Then both of the men began to beat him. His head, his back, his chest. I prayed that he would die.

They cut out his tongue. He fell to the floor, his blood soaking the carpet. Still, he didn't die.

Rommelmann suddenly turned to me.

"Let's find out what the little one knows."

He looked like death to me, death wearing shiny boots. I wished I were already dead.

He stood over me now.

"Where is the blue file? You know where your brother put those plans!"

They'll kill me, I thought, they'll kill me, too. I shook my head and began to sob.

"I don't know! I don't know! I don't know about any plans."

They hit me again and again, the way they had hit Romek.

"Where are those plans?" Rommelmann screamed. "Tell me!"

Finally, Grunow intervened.

"He doesn't know anything. He's too young."

All at once, I heard the silence. My brother wasn't screaming. God had answered his prayer . . . and mine. My mouth was too battered for speech, but in my mind I told Romek how much I loved him.

The men who had beaten him to death took me downstairs and out onto the street. I stumbled and almost fell. One of them grabbed my arm and shoved me into a car. They took me back to the ghetto gate and pushed me out.

I lay in the street, my eyes swollen shut from the beating. Two Jewish ghetto policemen came by. One bent over me and lifted my head.

"Who are you?" he asked. "What's your name?"

I opened my eyes and tried to speak.

"I'm David Faber," I mumbled.

"Were do you live, David? Can you tell me where you live?"

"Ulica Targowa 12."

They picked me up and carried me to the place where we lived and upstairs to the fourth floor.

Mother opened the door. She stared at me and then cried out.

"My God, David! What happened? What did they do to you? What did they do?"

I began sobbing. She took me in her arms, rocking back and forth. Finally, I stopped crying.

She held me at arm's length, and I knew she'd ask me about Romek. I didn't want to answer.

"Where is he?" Her voice trembled. "Where, David?"

I had never lied to Mama before. Never.

CHAPTER THIRTEEN

TARNÓW *We Got All of Them!*

Father and Romek were dead. Fella had returned to be with us. I was the head of the family, responsible for Mother and my sisters. That's what having a Bar Mitzvah meant, that I was a man. I felt like a man. The terror and sorrow of the past few months made everything about being a boy part of another world that was gone forever.

My mother kept looking at the note that Romek had left for her. She kept saying, "Come back to me, my Avrumaleh."[1] In the Yiddish language, that was her pet name for my brother. Romek was his nickname in Polish.

A few days after Romek's murder, Laika said, "I'm worried about Mama, David. She looks so tired. Sometimes she can hardly get her breath."

"I've noticed. I think it's her heart. We've got to get something for her to eat."

We had very little food now because the Germans wouldn't let anyone out of the ghetto except on work gangs. Laika made biscuits from flour I had found in an empty apartment on the ground floor, but it was almost gone. The Germans wanted us to starve.

Mother lay on her straw-filled sack for hours, usually with her eyes closed, now and then gasping for breath. When any of us spoke to her, asking how she felt or if she wanted some watery soup, she'd open her eyes and murmur, "I'm all right. I'm just thinking about Papa," or "I'm just thinking about Romek."

It hurt to see her like that. She had always taken care of us. Now we had to take care of her. I had to get more food.

"She'll die if we don't do something," I whispered to Laika one afternoon. "I'll go out tonight. I can get vegetables or something from the farmers we knew before the Germans put us in here."

"How can you?" Laika asked. "We don't have anything to trade."

"Almost all the apartments are empty now. I'll see if I can find something." I glanced at Mother lying with her eyes closed. "Don't tell Mama what I'm doing."

Quietly I opened the door and went down one flight of stairs. The first door on the left stood open, and I went in. There was a table and some overturned chairs, straw mattresses torn apart, bloodstains on the floor. The Germans had been here before me.

I turned and crossed the hall. Signs of death were here, too, but I made myself stay and search. Maybe a ring was hidden in the straw or under a loose board. I sifted the straw through my fingers. Nothing. Maybe taped to the bottom of the table? Again, nothing. I felt for loose floorboards, but there were none.

I had to find something. Maybe in the next apartment. This one looked better. Nothing was overturned or torn apart. Probably the people were shot or taken away while they were out on the street.

A real mattress lay against one wall. I bent over, picked up the thin blanket, shook it, listened for the sound of something hitting the floor. Nothing. I ran my hands over the top and sides of the mattress, feeling for a lump or a tear. Nothing. I turned it over and did the same. There! A tiny slit right along the edge. Jewelry could be hidden in that kind of place. My body tensed as I poked a finger through the hole. Then I felt something. Trembling, I tore open the mattress and pulled out the stuffing.

A small cloth bag, tied with a drawstring, fell onto the floor. I picked it up and held it for a moment before I loosened the string and turned the bag upside down over the mattress.

Jewelry tumbled out—rings, pins, some gold chains. I stirred them with my fingers and saw diamonds, pearls, and other stones I didn't know. They had to be real. No one would have hidden them otherwise.

Here was Mother's food! But maybe there was more. I kept looking. I tore apart the rest of the mattress, but I found nothing.

I ran my fingers along the floor, pushing every place two boards came together. I did the same with the walls. Behind a small picture, I found a board that moved when I pushed. I worked it free, put my hand inside the small hole, and found a nail with a cord hanging from it. I pulled and felt a weight. Carefully, I drew on the cord until something caught against the nail. I put my hand on what felt like another cloth bag, freed it from the nail and brought it out through the hole.

It was bigger than the first one and heavier. More jewelry spilled out as I shook it above the mattress. Now there was plenty.

I poured the jewelry back into the bags, thinking about the people who hid it. They must be dead or in a labor camp. I had never seen them, but I imagined they were older to have owned so much. I wished I could let them know that another person, another Jew, was helped by it. I was sure they would feel good.

Suddenly I couldn't stand the emptiness of that room and what it meant. I ran out, clutching the bags, and hurried back upstairs.

Mother was lying as I had left her.

"She didn't know you were gone," Laika said.

She saw the bags in my hands. "What did you find?"

"Look," I said, as I emptied the bags onto the floor. "I can go for food tonight."

Sonia picked up a diamond ring and slipped it on her finger. She was so thin that it fell off as she held out her hand to admire it.

"Don't play with those things!" I yelled at her. "You might lose something."

"I'm sorry, I'm sorry. They're so pretty -" She began to cry softly.

I hugged her, ashamed of what I had done.

"It's all right, Sonia. It's all right. Here, look at all of them. Just be careful."

She wiped her eyes and smiled. "I'll be careful, David."

"Are you sure you can get out, David?" Laika asked. "And back in again?"

"I'm pretty sure. I have to try. We can't just let Mama die."

"You're right. You have to go."

"If I get caught, what difference does it make?" I asked. "We'll all die here without food, anyway."

I lay awake until about midnight, thinking about how I would sneak out of the ghetto and where I would get food. I'd go to the farm closest to Tarnów, where Mother and I had gone several times before. The old farmer there was cranky, but his wife was nice. She'd let me in, I thought.

Straw rustled as Laika turned on her bed. I got up, knelt beside her, and whispered, "I'm going now."

"Be careful," she whispered back and kissed my cheek. "May God protect you."

Once outside the building, I hurried to a spot I knew, where there was a little space under the barbed wire. Being as skinny as I was, I didn't need much room. I lay on the ground at the side of a building, waiting for the guard to go past. In a few minutes, I saw him coming, his rifle on his shoulder, not paying much attention to anything. When he moved out of sight, I slid under the fence and hurried through the dark streets. Everything was quiet in the city and along the dirt road that led to the farm.

I'd have to be at the fence again before morning, before it got light. I ran as fast as I could, stumbling now and then on a rough place. Just before I reached the farm, I tripped and fell hard. I felt a sharp pain as my right knee hit against a rock, but I got up and went on, limping a little.

It was an hour or more after midnight, and the farmhouse was dark. I went to the kitchen door and knocked as hard as I could. No answer. I knocked again.

I heard footsteps inside the house, and through the window I saw the flickering light of a candle moving toward the door.

Then the old man grumbled, "Who is it? What do you want?"

"It's David Faber. Remember? My mother and I traded with you for food. Please let me in."

"Go away! Come in the daytime!"

"I can't come then. The Nazis won't let us out. Please open the door."

"No! Go away!"

Then I heard his wife's voice.

"Let him in, Janos. He's just a boy. It's dangerous for him to be out there. Let him in."

The old man muttered something I couldn't hear, then he drew back the bolt and opened the door.

"Come in, quick!" he said.

I stepped inside, and he closed the door behind me. He held the candle in front of my face.

"Yes, I remember you. Why did you come in the middle of the night?"

"They won't let us out. I had to slip out in the dark. I have to get food. My mother is very sick, and we don't have anything for her to eat. Please help us. I've got jewelry to trade."

He stroked his sparse, pointed beard and looked down at me with his watery eyes. I wondered why he was so thin when he had plenty to eat.

The woman brought a lighted lamp from another room and set it on a worn table. Short and plump, she was very different from her tall husband. He always seemed angry, while she had a warm smile and a kind manner.

"Look at you," she said. "Your leg is all bloody. What happened? Let me see."

There was a big cut just below my kneecap, and blood had run all the way down my leg.

"I fell and hit a rock," I told her.

"I'll clean it up and put on a bandage."

I sat on a chair and held out my leg. The woman went to the hand pump at one end of the long, stone sink and drew water into an enameled pan. Then she turned to her husband.

"Janos, go get two chickens."

"I want to see what he has to trade, first," he grumbled. "Maybe it's not worth much."

"It's all good," I said. "Diamonds and pearls and gold chains. Here, I'll show you."

I pulled a bag out of my pocket and emptied it on the table. Janos looked at the rings, then picked up a chain and bit it.

"It's gold." He turned and went outside.

The woman finished bandaging my leg and set the pan on the table.

"You must be hungry," she said. "I'll warm some milk and *kluskis*[2] for you."

She stirred the smoldering fire in the brick stove and added chunks of coal, then poured milk and dumplings into a small pot and placed it on the burner. In a few minutes, she filled a bowl, set the steaming food in front of me, and patted my shoulder.

The first spoonful of hot broth burned my tongue, and I put my hand over my mouth.

She laughed. "Let it cool a little," she said.

I nodded and stirred the food, then sipped a second spoonful. Its warmth moved down my throat and into my stomach. Nothing I ever ate tasted better. Then I bit into a *kluski*, a round ball rich with the flavor of butter and eggs. I ate slowly, to make the food last.

Before I finished, Janos came back to the kitchen, a headless chicken dangling from each hand. He gave one hen to his wife and dumped the other one on the stone sink. Blood tricked from its neck and ran across the sink.

The sight would have upset my stomach a few months before. Now I had seen things so much worse that it didn't bother me. I kept on eating until I had emptied the bowl.

"That was good," I told the woman. "Thank you."

"I've fixed some other things for you to take back." She wrapped butter in paper, then put it and some eggs into a big, enamel cup. From the cupboard, she took two round loaves of bread. She stuffed the chickens into a cloth sack and put potatoes and carrots on top of them. Finally, she put in the butter and eggs.

"You'd better start back," she said as she handed the sack to me. "It will be light soon."

"Yes," I said, "but could I have one more thing, please? I need sugar to put Mother's medicine on."

"All right," she nodded and smiled. She wrapped sugar cubes in a cloth and put that in the bag with the other things.

"That's enough," Janos said. "That's all the jewelry is worth."

I slung the bag over my shoulder and went to the door. The woman opened it and patted my back as I started outside.

"Be careful," she said. "God go with you."

"Shut the door," Janos growled.

How different they are, I thought. Both of them hate the Germans. I know that from what they've said before. But all Janos seems to care about is how much gold he can get for his food. His wife is so different. She acts like she cares what happens to us.

I walked to the city, afraid to run because of the load I carried.

It was still dark when I came to the ghetto fence, and I felt relief at being almost back to the apartment. All I had to do was slide under again and then go a little farther.

I lay down on my back and slid beneath the wire, then pulled the sack after me. Instead of coming along, it caught on the barbs. I tugged to get it loose. That made it worse. I tried to loosen it, feeling for the barbs, the sharp points poking into my fingers.

I didn't know how long it would be before the guard passed by again. I had to get the sack loose. I couldn't fail now, when I'd almost gotten home. My stomach cramped, and I felt warm urine running down my legs.

The guard might be coming any minute. I yanked as hard as I could, and I felt the sack tear. Finally, it moved, sliding to my side of the fence. I got to my feet and tried to run. Sharp stomach pains doubled me over. I half-walked, half-crawled into an empty building and collapsed on the floor.

The cramps were worse now. They felt like they were tearing out my insides. I lay there, unable to control my bowels, too sick to move.

It's the *kluskis*, I thought. They were too much, and I'm so tired and scared. But I got back with the food! I'll be all right. I've got to get to the apartment before it's light.

The cramps got weaker, and I forced myself to get up and start walking. It was only a couple of blocks to our building, and in a few minutes I climbed the stairs and tapped on our door.

Laika opened it.

"Thank God you're back," she said. "Did you get food?"

"Yes. Enough for a little while."

I handed her the sack and watched while she emptied it.

"It's wonderful," she said. "Oh, David, you're such a good boy. You're the baby of the family; we should be taking care of you, and here you are taking care of us."

"I'm not a baby anymore," I answered.

Laika and Sabina heated water and plucked the hens, then boiled them and made soup, good soup with big chunks of meat floating in it.

Mother opened her eyes and looked at us.

"Look, Mama," I said. "The girls made some good soup for you, and we have eggs, too."

Mother looked puzzled. "Where did it come from?"

"From the farm where you and I used to go," I told her. "I got it for you to make you well."

She smiled and closed her eyes.

Laika crushed sugar cubes, mixed them with egg yolks, and whipped them until they were foamy—an old family remedy. She took the bowl and knelt by Mother.

"Mama," Laika spoke softly. "Mama, here's something good for you." She turned to me. "Help Mama sit up, David, please."

I put my arm around Mother's shoulders and raised her as gently as I could.

"Look, Mama," I said, "see what we've fixed for you."

Laika filled a spoon with the egg yolks and pressed it against Mother's lips.

"Open your mouth, please, Mama," she said.

Mother opened her mouth, and my sister fed her, spoonful by spoonful, until she had eaten it all. I took away my arm and let her lie back on the straw. After she had rested a while, we brought soup and fed her in the same way. She needed medicine, but we had nothing except some valerian[3] drops. I had traded my Omega watch, a Bar Mitzvah present, for the medicine the day before. Laika put three drops on a cube of sugar and placed it in Mother's mouth every few hours.

As she became stronger, Mother ate the chunks of chicken and little by little became almost well again.

It was quiet for a few days, then early one morning boots crashed against the thin, wooden door and broke it open. I slid under our ragged sofa, but Mother and my sisters had no time to hide.

Before I thought about what was happening, rifle shots deafened me. Then all was quiet. The smell of gunpowder filled the room. Flat on my back, I peered out. Two booted feet were a few inches from my head; another pair moved across the room. The soldier next to me stepped away, and I saw bodies lying on the floor. Three bodies—Mother, Sabina, and Sonia.

I closed my eyes and tried to shut out the world. Dimly, I heard voices saying something in German and someone laughing. I felt something hitting me, hard, again and again. One of the soldiers jumped up and down on the sofa, banking its sagging springs against my stomach. Each time he landed on the worn cushions, vomit rose in my throat and mouth. I couldn't lift my head to spit it out, couldn't wipe my face. Desperately, I tried not to gag or grunt as the springs slammed into my middle.

The pounding stopped, and I heard a loud voice.

"We got all of them! We cleaned them out!"

"*Ja!*" a second voice echoed satisfaction.

I heard the thud of boots hitting the floor as the first soldier jumped off the sofa. The footsteps faded into silence as the two of them went out and down the stairs.

I lay still for a few minutes to be sure they were gone. Slowly I slid from my hiding place, spit out vomit, and wiped my face. I didn't look at the bodies as I walked across the room, dipped a cup into the bucket of water by the stove, and rinsed my mouth.

I turned and looked at my mother and my sisters. Now I saw not three but six bodies: Mama, Sonia, Sabina, Laika, Kreindel, and Fella. I felt no grief, no loss, no anger. I felt nothing. I didn't care who these people were or what had happened to them. I thought I should care, but I couldn't. There was no feeling left inside me. I lay down on the sofa and went to sleep.

It was dark when I awoke. For a moment, I couldn't remember why it was so quiet. Then it came back to me. All were dead. Only I was left. I began to cry, quietly at first, then with deeper sobs. Finally, exhausted, I fell into uneasy sleep, tormented by dreams of Father's battered face and of the poker jammed into Romek's eye.

CHAPTER FOURTEEN

SZEBNIA *The Promise and the "Heidelager"*

In the morning I awoke, remembering everything. I lay on the sofa, dreading being alone. Hunger forced me to get up, and I ate a piece of bread, almost the last I had brought from the farm. I filled my stomach with water.

I knelt beside Mama and touched her cold face with my fingertips. Her open eyes stared up at me, commanding me to survive. But what was there to live for?

I pulled Sonia gently off Mama, and suddenly remembered something Sonia had told me just a few days before. The two of us had been sitting near our makeshift stove, waiting for some potatoes to bake, when she had begun to cry. "I've never been kissed by a boy," she had said. "I'll never get married." She and I always used to tell each other secrets.

Now Sonia was dead. I kissed her and said, "I'm so sorry, my dear Zhendele," using my pet name for her.

I lay down on top of Mama, put my arms beneath her stiff body, and held her close. "I promise you, Mama, I'll live. I'll survive, and I'll go to London and find Rachel. I'll tell the world what they've done to us. I will, Mama, I promise."

I wet a rag and wiped away the blood. Then I covered each of them with a white cloth. I could do that for them.

I lost track of time. Sometimes it was light, and sometimes it was dark. When it was light, I got up and ate a little. And I drank a lot of water.

The smell of dead bodies filled the apartment. I didn't want to leave Mother and the girls. It seemed like deserting them. But I couldn't stay. I decided to go down to the apartment where I had found the jewelry. I could lie on the mattress there.

Soon the last bits of food were gone. There was only water. Then that was shut off.

Then I heard loudspeakers blaring German words.

"Alle Juden raus! Das Wasser ist abgestellt." Over and over, the same command. "All Jews come out! The water is turned

110

off!"

If I stayed inside, I would die of thirst. If I went out, there was at least a chance to survive. And I had promised Mama.

I forced myself up from the mattress where I had lain most of the past two days. During that time, I had moved only to relieve myself in a corner of the back room; but with no water or food for days, there was not much need for that.

Slowly I moved toward the door, opened it, and went out into the hall. I stopped at the stairs, the harsh German words like blows to my face. Then I started down, made myself lift one foot and let it fall on the step below, then lift the other.

The noise stopped before I got all the way down, then rifle shots came again. I opened the door and looked out. An old man came from the building across the street, his hands on top of his head. A soldier standing on the sidewalk near my door lifted his machine gun and fired. The old man staggered back a step or two, then fell to the ground. People nearby looked away.

I stood inside the door. They'd probably shoot me, too. Maybe I should have stayed upstairs, but I didn't want to starve to death or die of thirst.

I put my hands on my head and stepped onto the sidewalk. The soldier who had shot the old man pointed his gun at me. I was sure he was going to shoot. Instead, he swung the gun barrel toward the middle of the street and yelled, "Run!"

With my hands still on my head, I ran as fast as I could the few steps to where several people huddled together. I clipped behind two men and waited, shivering in the cold air.

More people came out until there were almost a hundred of us. Old men and women, some alone, a few clinging to one another; younger women holding small children in their arms or close against them.

A child, four or five years old, stood next to me. In one hand she held a china doll. The other clung to the hand of an old woman. The little girl whispered something to her doll, then looked up at me. Tears streaked her thin face.

I smiled at her. "What's your dolly's name?" I asked.

She stared at me for a long time, then answered, "Ruth. Ruth's afraid. Her stomach hurts."

I didn't want to tell her I was afraid, too. Instead, I touched her dark braids.

"You have pretty hair," I told her. "Did your mama braid it?"

"My mama and papa went away," she answered. "Babcia[1] takes care of me."

The old woman turned to me.

"We're all that's left," she said. "And you?"

"Just me."

I tried to stay near the middle so the soldiers couldn't hit me as they walked around the edges. After a half hour or so, no more people came out. One of the soldiers shouted at us to move down the street.

All around me, people shuffled along, too weak to hurry. Every now and then, a soldier hit someone on the head or shoulders, yelling, "Move faster!" An old woman limped along in front of me, stumbling as a loose sole on one shoe caught on the pavement.

We came to ulica Lwowska, on the other side of the ghetto, where there was a round, open space like a market. Hundreds of people already stood there, in rows of five. We lined up with them, soldiers with machine guns and rifles all around us.

"They're going to kill us!" The grandmother's voice shook as she gripped my arm. I thought so, too.

A truck drove up and stopped in front of us. Two soldiers got out and stood behind it. The back was uncovered, and I saw blankets and tall wooden boxes that looked like outdoor toilets.

A sergeant yelled at us to walk by the truck. As we did, one soldier handed each person a thin, grey blanket. The other demanded our names and wrote them in a book he held against the side of the truck. Jews unloaded the tall boxes and put them in a row at one side of the street. They really were outhouses.

The sergeant looked up and down the rows. "Anybody who goes back inside will be shot!"

Another truck drove up, this one with big kettles. I could see steam rising from them. It must be food, I thought. A soldier yelled at three men to take the big, red bowls piled by the kettles and hand one to each of us as we filed past the truck.

I took my bowl and shuffled ahead. When I reached the kettle, I held out the bowl with both hands, wanting to be sure nothing spilled. The hot soup warmed my fingers as I lifted the bowl and sniffed. I could feel heat against my face, but there wasn't any smell.

The man ahead of me turned and asked, "Young fellow, do you know how to swim?"

"No."

"What a shame! You could dive in and see if you could find a potato."

He laughed, patted my shoulder, and walked away.

It was almost tasteless, but after three days without food, the soup helped fill my stomach.

When the soup was finished, I wrapped myself in the blanket and lay down on the street, drawing my legs up against my chest. All around, others sat huddled over or lay curled on their sides. As it got colder, people began to move toward one another until we were pressed together, sharing the warmth our bodies offered.

I slept a little. I heard racking coughs, children crying, and an old woman wailing most of the night. Daylight came and with it the soldiers, shouting at us to get up, poking us with their bayonets.

Sore and stiff, I scrambled to my feet and got into a line to use the outhouse.

A truck came with our breakfast of black coffee and a slice of bread. A second one brought many two-wheeled pushcarts. Soldiers jumped from both trucks and ordered some men to hand out the coffee and bread. Others unloaded the pushcarts. When everyone was fed, a sergeant counted us off into groups of eight. Two soldiers guarded each group.

My group was ordered to go to a building on ulica Lwowka and to strip each apartment of everything in it. We started on the top floor and worked our way down. It didn't matter if a chair or table was broken; everything had to be carried down the stairs and left on the sidewalk. Trucks came by, and other work parties loaded them. I suppose the Germans took for themselves anything that was worthwhile and burned the rest or dumped it.

Now and then, we found dead bodies. We carried them

downstairs, too, and put them on a cart. We pushed the carts to the ghetto entrance and loaded the bodies onto trucks. That's what happened to Mother and my sisters.

Every day was the same. Soldiers woke us up at dawn. We'd have coffee and a slice of bread, and go back to stripping the apartments. Late in the afternoon, we'd have soup, then try to stay alive through the night. The only changes were that it snowed sometimes, and our number got smaller. As the weeks passed, more and more people died, their half-frozen bodies the first to be loaded onto the carts each day.

One day about two months later, the soldiers got us up and held roll call, but ordered us to leave the dead where they lay. We didn't have coffee and bread. Instead, we stood for an hour or more in rows of five. If a soldier saw someone turn or shift his feet, he hit the person on the shoulders with his rifle butt or stabbed his buttocks with the bayonet.

Time dragged by. I was hot then cold, then hot again. In the row in front of me, a man's head seemed to move in circles, and I began to sway.

Engines roared. A truck turned around the corner, followed by an open army car and a second truck. Two soldiers sat in the front of the car; a Gestapo officer sat alone in the back.

I knew the man. His name was Faber, the same as mine. He was my mother's customer! He bought lemons for his little grocery store in Katowice. I knew he had joined the Nazis, but I didn't know that this *Reichsdeutscher*,[2] this nobody, was now a colonel, one of the highest-ranking Nazis in Tarnów. Instead of selling groceries, he now controlled our lives.

The officer got out of the car, his pudgy figure almost hidden by the soldiers. He raised his hand, and two of them brought a heavy, wooden platform from a truck. He stomped up the three steps and put his hands on his hips. His blue eyes stared straight ahead.

"You have committed a crime," he shouted. "You were told to come out of the buildings, and you did not obey. You are going to be punished. You must learn to obey."

Frowning, he touched his finger to the underside of his blond moustache. "I'm going to give you the surprise of your life," he said.

I wondered how the punishment could be worse than what we had already suffered.

A few minutes later, another truck drove up. Soldiers jumped out, holding machine guns in front of them. The Gestapo colonel watched as they surrounded us. Then he held his right arm straight out, almost like the Nazi solute. His hand dropped, and the soldiers opened fire.

My knees buckled, and I fell to the ground.

The next thing I knew, I heard a quiet voice.

"Son, how badly are you wounded?"

I opened my eyes. A man knelt beside me, holding my head in his hands. I looked at him for a moment before answering. He was about fifty, short and thin, with a small, pointed, black beard.

"Wounded?" I didn't know what he was talking about.

"They shot every second person. I thought you were one of them."

"I don't feel anything. I think I just fainted. My knees gave way, and I fell down."

"God has saved you. He wants you to live. That's why you fainted."

I didn't answer for a moment.

Then I said, "Yes, I have to live. I promised Mama."

By the time I got to my feet, the man had walked away.

People lay in uneven lines all over the street, a few still alive. Heads moved; arms rose and dropped. Nearby, a woman held a child in her bloody arms. Two old men stood side by side, hands in front, nodding in prayer. I looked for the little girl with the doll. I didn't see her.

I saw Faber walking back to his car, looking pleased. I hated him. I wanted to kill him. He got into the car and rode away.

After a few minutes, more trucks came, and the soldiers yelled at us to load the bodies. I didn't move until I saw a rifle butt swung at my head. I ducked, and it slammed against my shoulder, knocking me to my knees.

"Schwein!" the soldier screamed.

I struggled to my feet, holding my injured arm with the other hand, and hurried to help pick up the dead. There were more than three hundred of them. One of them was the little girl.

By the time we finished, it was mid-afternoon or later. They made us stand again, not moving, soldiers all around us, through the rest of the day and until almost morning.

Just before dawn, I heard the noise of engines again. This time, it sounded like many trucks. I thought they were coming to kill the rest of us. It might be better if they did, I thought.

The headlights of the first truck swept around the corner. More followed, about six or eight. The first one stopped in front of us, and the driver turned off the engine.

A Gestapo officer got out and shouted, "Get these *Schweine* into the trucks!"

The soldiers began yelling at us. Those with rifles jabbed their bayonets into whatever bodies they could reach. One of them jabbed into my leg, and I began to cry.

Bodies pressed against me, pushing me toward one of the trucks. My chest hit against the truck bed, and I felt as though my ribs were being crushed. Someone behind me grabbed my waist and lifted, scraping me along the metal edge. I got hold of a corner post and pulled myself to my feet.

More people followed, jamming my face against the bodies in front of me. There was an awful smell. Nobody had bathed for two months, and the odor of urine and other excretions nauseated me. It was a cold day, but the heat of so many bodies became almost unbearable.

Taller people pushed against me. I turned my face to one side, trying to breathe. Behind me, a man leaned on my sore shoulder, making my arm throb. Suddenly he threw up, vomit spilling down the back of my head. As we rode for several hours, I stood, unable to clean myself. The stench grew worse, and I kept swallowing to keep from vomiting.

The truck made a sharp turn and stopped. I heard dogs barking, men shouting. The truck jerked ahead and stopped again. Two men took off the tailgate and yelled at us to get off. With the others I shuffled to the rear and half-jumped, half-fell onto the ground.

It was just like the ghetto—soldiers with machine guns surrounding us. But they looked different, not like Germans. Their faces were broad, and their eyes looked smaller. They screamed at us to do something, but no one understood them because their German was so bad. They became angrier and started beating us with their rifles.

Then the dogs were let loose to bite and tear at us. I wore two pairs of pants and two shirts. That's what Mama told me to do after the Nazis put us in the ghetto.

"We might have to leave," she had said, "and this way you'll have extra clothes."

A dog ran at me, barking and snarling. I jumped, but its teeth went through both pairs of pants and into the calf of my right leg. The dog jerked its head from side to side, and I could feel the flesh tear. Then it turned and attacked someone else.

I pulled up my pants leg and saw blood streaming down into my shoe. I took off my outer shirt, tore away a sleeve, and tied it around my leg as tightly as I could.

Gradually we understood that the guards wanted us to get into rows of five. It seemed that's what they always wanted. Maybe it was easier to count us that way. I limped into a row near the front and stood there, hurting all over.

A few minutes later, a very tall Gestapo officer stepped out from behind the guards. He must have been at least six and a half feet tall, a broad-shouldered giant with blond hair brushed straight back, green eyes, and thin lips.

He began talking, not shouting like the others always did, but instead using an almost quiet monotone.

"I am *Hauptsturmführer* Grzymek," he said. "Welcome to Szebnia.[3] You are lucky! You are in a vacation camp."

Suddenly he leaned forward and screamed at us, waving his right arm up and down.

"If you obey orders, you'll be fine! You'll enjoy it here because you're under my wing, and I am like an angel for you. But remember! I tell you when to live and when to die! I decide your destiny! If you break the rules, you'll die!"

He stopped talking and walked up and down the rows, pushing

people to one side or the other. He shoved me to the left, along with young men and women and older children. Old people and little children had to go to the right. They climbed back onto the trucks and went out of the camp.

The guards forced us into a wooden barrack, where we had to strip and stand under icy water that poured down from rows of pipes that ran the length of the building. We had no soap, no towels. I had never been naked in front of strangers before, and I felt ashamed.

Dripping wet, we went into a second room. Guards pulled old clothes from big, wooden boxes with rope handles and threw them at us. Nobody cared if anything fit, as long as you could get it on.

I still had the loaf of rye bread Mama gave me. Part of the top was missing because she had cut out a piece, put a gold chain inside the loaf, and covered it with the soft part. The chain was her wedding gift from my father. The guards grabbed the bread from my hands and tore it apart, laughing at the sight of so much gold.

Finally, we marched into a very long barrack, with rows of beds, three high on each side of a narrow center aisle. Seven people slept on each bunk, lying on the bare boards without even a sack of straw for a mattress. There were no blankets.

I climbed onto a bottom bunk and lay there, eyes closed, wanting to forget where I was. Other prisoners lay down next to me, but I didn't open my eyes to look at them. Dark came early in late November, and I soon fell asleep.

Guards burst in at five o'clock the next morning, yelling at us to get up. As we got out of the bunks, they continued to yell. "Stand straight! Hold your hats!" I understood them, but many people didn't. They saw a few of us standing stiff, hats in our hands, and I did the same—but not quickly enough to escape the guards' blows and curses.

The guards counted us, but the number was short. Two men had died during the night. This was the way every day began.

We stayed in the barrack for two days, doing nothing. Every morning we had black coffee and a piece of bread, with no more food for the rest of the day. Then a sergeant came and assigned jobs to each of us: to clean the camp, sweep the barracks, dig ditches, build fences. My job was to help build a fence around the kitchen.

Some of the other workers had been in the camp for a long time. We weren't allowed to talk, but we did when we thought the guards weren't looking.

"Where did you come from?" one man whispered to me.

"Katowice," I answered. "And Tarnów."

"Cracow," he said.

Five or six thousand people were in Szebnia, from every city in that part of Poland. It was supposed to be a work camp, not a concentration camp. That's why old people and little children had been sent somewhere else.

A boy about my own age slept in the same bunk. His name was Sammy. He was as short as I, but chubby. He had a full face and dark hair and eyes. Before the war, he had lived in Cracow with his parents and three younger sisters. Now, just like me, he had lost them all. His father was a tailor, and Sammy's constant lament was, "They took away the beautiful suit my father made for me for Passover holidays."

We were drawn to each other at once, each needing someone with whom to share his grief and loneliness. At night, we lay side by side and talked about our families, about how good life had been. We talked, too, about what might happen next and promised each other we would live and be friends after the war.

After we had been in camp for about a week, the guards came in early one morning as usual, but this time they ordered us to stand outside in rows of five. Other guards with machine guns were all around, and Grzymek, our "angel," stood with his hands behind his back.

He began shouting as soon as we were lined up.

"You drew a lucky ticket, and you don't know how to behave! Look how well off you are! Still you broke a lot of rules! I have to teach you a lesson!"

Nobody knew what rules we had broken. We knew it didn't make any difference what we did. Grzymek would punish us simply because he wanted to.

He picked out five young girls, their thin faces beautiful even in this terrible place.

"Shoot them!" he screamed.

The girls lay on the ground, blood spotting their ragged clothes.

"You must obey," Grzymek quietly said, then he turned and walked away.

This was the "*Heidelager*," the "vacation camp."

Shortly after roll call one morning, Sammy and I were sitting on the bunk. For a change, we didn't have a job to do.

"Let's go outside," I said. "I hate it in here."

A guard shouted at us as soon as we stepped through the door. "*Komm her!* Over here!"

Sammy didn't understand and kept walking.

I grabbed his arm. "Wait! He's telling us to come. Let's go. Take off your hat and bow. That's what they want."

Sammy did as I told him. We both looked down and bowed.

"Where are you going?"

"Just for a walk," I answered.

"So, you think you came here to walk, eh? Come with me!"

He took us to a shed, where he got shovels, and then to another building.

"They want a fence around this kitchen," he said. "Dig post holes, one and one-half feet wide and three feet deep."

"*Jawohl!*" I answered.

We started digging. Sammy pushed the shovel beneath a rock, pushed hard, and broke the handle. He looked at me with tears in his eyes.

"What will they do to me?" he whispered.

"Maybe they'll just hit you, Sammy." I tried to reassure him. "It's an old shovel. The handle was already split."

He tried to keep on digging, but it was even harder with only the stub—especially as the holes got deeper. Before we finished, the guard returned.

"Why aren't the holes finished?" he demanded.

Sammy seemed to shrink as he held out the shovel. "It broke," he said in Polish. "I'm sorry."

"You've sabotaged German property," the guard screamed at him. "I'll teach you!"

He dragged Sammy to the center of the camp, where roll call

was held. A tall pole with a hook near the top stood in the middle of the open space. Another guard came with a rope, and the first one tied Sammy's hands behind his back. Then they lifted him up and slipped the rope over the hook. It was about nine in the morning.

I kept on digging. Every time I looked up, I could see Sammy hanging there, screaming in pain. After a half hour or so, his hands turned black, then his arms and face.

All day long, I heard him cry for someone to kill him.

"Please," he'd twist his head to look at me. "Please, kill me! Cut my throat! Kill me, please!"

Over and over, the same plea. That's all I could hear. I cried as I worked, filled with hate. If only I could do something to save Sammy! I knew I couldn't. They'd kill me, too, and Sammy would still hang there. All this over only a shovel with a broken handle!

A little after four, there was another roll call. The whole camp gathered in the open space around that awful pole. Sammy was still alive, but his screaming had stopped.

Grzymek strode to the front of the group and looked up at Sammy. He started shouting.

"You still don't know how lucky you are! You're still going against my rules! I'll show you what happens when you sabotage German property!"

He pulled a revolver with a long barrel from the holster on his belt and shot Sammy in the face. Blood ran down his blackened face, but he still lived. Grzymek smiled and stepped away.

He shouted at us again. "The devil! Look at him! He's still living. What power you Jews have! I'll break that power for you!"

He walked back and put a bullet into Sammy's brain. My friend was at peace.

Two guards took him down, and he fell on his face. They let me and two others pick him up and take him to a corner of our barrack that pretended to be a "clinic." Later his body was taken away.

That night, I lay on the bunk weeping for Sammy and for myself. His agony was over, but mine went on. I had lost another brother. I was alone again.

The following day, I was assigned a job not far from the gate.

Suddenly, in the early afternoon, I heard shooting. I fell face-down on the frozen ground.

I heard more shots and guards' voices shouting. I looked up and saw the gates open and men in civilian clothes running into the camp. There seemed to be seven or eight of them. In Polish, German, and Hebrew, they yelled, "We're partisans! You're going to be free!"

Two army trucks roared through the gate, and soldiers with machine guns jumped out. All the partisans were killed. It happened so fast, that I didn't feel despair. There wasn't time to think about getting away until it was finished. About a week later, a larger group, twenty-five or thirty men, tried to liberate us. Again, they all were killed.

I felt good that somebody cared about me and the others, but there was no hope. The Nazis were too strong. There were too many of them. We'd never get away.

At roll call a few days later, we knew something bad was going to happen. Twice as many guards surrounded us, and we saw soldiers and trucks outside the gates. Grzymek stomped up the three steps and stood on the wooden box, staring down at us for several minutes.

"You *Schweine* are lucky!" he shouted. "You've drawn another lucky ticket!"

He paused and bared his teeth in a terrible smile. I wondered dully who would be killed this time.

"You're going to another vacation camp! You're so lucky!" He laughed, got down from the box, and walked away.

We stood there all day in the snow, no food, no water. After an hour or so, the man in front of me began wavering back and forth, then collapsed like a bundle of dirty rags. As time passed, I saw more lying where they fell, unconscious or dead.

The dead were free, like Sammy. Like my family. That was better. No, I told myself. You can't give up. I tried to empty my mind, not think of anything, just stand and wait, in a kind of trance.

Grzymek's voice brought me back to reality. I opened my eyes. For a moment, the tall figure standing on the box seemed like an evil spirit, a dybbuk.[4] Well, he was a devil.

"Empty your pockets!" he yelled. "Drop everything on the ground in front of you. Everything! If you keep anything, you'll be shot!"

Money, gold, all kinds of jewelry came out of the ragged clothes. I knew people kept valuables they'd found on the dead bodies in the ghetto. And they had swallowed things before they were stripped when they came to the camp, or they had hidden them in their bodies. But I couldn't believe the fortune that lay on the ground.

Guards walked between the rows of prisoners, picking up their treasures from the dirty snow and stuffing them into cloth sacks. I wondered how many things went into their own pockets.

It must have been after midnight when the guards began shouting at us to go outside the gate. There we climbed into the trucks and rode until we came to a train station, probably near Tarnów.

A long train of freight wagons stood there, reaching into the dark beyond the lighted platform. Soldiers herded us onto the train, at least a hundred persons packed like sardines in each wagon. There was no room to sit, not even to move. The only air came through a little opening high in one wall, about two feet wide and eighteen inches high, with barbed wire strung across it.

A young man pressed against the side of the wagon near me somehow tore loose the barbed wire and moved it to one side. He pulled himself up to the opening, squeezed his body through, and disappeared. A few minutes later, another man followed, and another and another, falling into the dark. Young women, too, worked their way across the crowded wagon and escaped through the window.

An older man standing beside me muttered, "I wish I had the guts to do that. I don't know where to run. But I know where we're going. I'll bet we're going to Auschwitz."

I didn't answer. Instead, I suddenly thought, "Oh, God, now I can sit down!" I slid down the side wall and slumped on the floor.

Days and nights passed as the train dragged on and on. Now and then it would stop, then with a jerk start again. Four days with no food, no water. I didn't think I could last much longer. Many people in the wagon were dead or only half-alive. There was no one to talk to, nothing to hope for.

The train stopped again. I looked out of a window at the top of the wall of the boxcar. In the glare of floodlights, I saw a gate and above it a sign that read *Arbeit Macht Frei*—Work Makes Free.

Photo by Richard Reck

This photo [2004] shows the entrance gate at Auschwitz. The camp has been preserved as a museum and a memorial.

CHAPTER FIFTEEN

Auschwitz *Number 161051*

The train started to move again. The wheels scraped against the rails as the train moved ahead through the open gate below that huge sign, and stopped. I heard footsteps on the gravel and shouts in German. Guards must be surrounding the train, I thought, but I was too short to see them.

A heavy voice shouted, "Open the door!"

The door slid open a few inches, then all the way as hands pushed against it. Soldiers stood outside with machine guns. Men in striped, prison uniforms climbed into the wagon, carrying long, wooden bats.

"Get out, you *Schweine*! Get out of here!"

They came toward us from the door, swinging the bats. Those who could get to their feet tried to dodge the blows. The guards swung the bats and pieces of heavy rubber hose with cable inside that hurt even more.

I thought we would step onto a platform. Instead, there was a drop of about four feet. People stepped onto nothing and fell, screaming as they piled on top of one another.

When I got to the door, I jumped as far as I could. One foot hit the pile of bodies, and I sprawled on the ground. Knees bruised and hands scraped, I scrambled to my feet.

When the living were out of the train, the guards jumped from it and beat those who lay jumbled together on the ground. Some never got up.

Huge floodlights lit the area. Our wagon was almost the last one in the long train reaching beyond the station platform. That was why people had fallen. I looked the other way toward the engine. Thousands of people were on the platform or moving toward it. Some stumbled and lay where they fell. Others tried to dodge the soldiers' rifle butts. Dogs snarled and lunged at prisoners along the edges of the crowd.

Suddenly, I grunted and stumbled as something hit me hard on the ribs.

"Run! *Kleiner Schweinehund!* You dirty little pig-dog!" The soldier pointed toward the front of the train.

I ran and climbed up the platform steps. An SS officer paced up and down at the far end. When we were in rows of five, he stepped onto a box and shouted, "*Ich bin Hauptsturmführer Schwartz.* Do what I tell you, or you'll wish you had!"

We waited. Just like at Szebnia, the dogs bit us, tearing clothes and flesh. There was no way to escape them. If anyone moved, a soldier beat him back into line.

Soon, big trucks roared up and parked along the platform. Each one had a big, round tank on the side, like a boiler.

Another SS officer walked along the rows, tapping a piece of cable against his left palm. He'd shout, "You go to the left!" or "You go to the right!" and swing the cable hard against the person. Those he sent to the left were forced into the trucks. Thousands were hauled away, until only a few hundred of us stood under the floodlights.

Finally, the colonel ordered us to march straight ahead, down the steps at the end of the platform. We walked for what seemed almost an hour. My side ached, and I was so weak I could barely lift my feet.

We stopped in front of a huge barrack. Guards ordered the first rows to go inside, and a few minutes later, the screams began. We whispered to one another, afraid of some new punishment.

My row was ordered inside. A fat guard stood close to the door. "Take off your clothes!" he yelled.

I stripped, and a taller guard grabbed my arm. With the other hand, he ran a hand clipper back and forth over my head until I was bald. It was nearly wintertime—November 1943—and extremely cold. I stood in the long line, naked and shivering.

It was almost morning when I reached the front of the line. A guard took hold of my arm and jerked me toward him.

I winced and made a face as he jabbed a pen into my wrist.

The man grinned. "You don't like it?" he asked.

He slapped my face with his open hand, knocking out two front teeth. Blood spurted from my nose and mouth.

"You think this hurts? Just wait! You know where you are?"

"No, sir."

"You're in Auschwitz. What did you think you came for, a vacation? This is where we'll get rid of you, you bastard!"

He stabbed the pen deep into my flesh, yanked it out, and stuck it back in, again and again. Every time he pulled it out, I prayed it was the end. My arm hurt so much I forgot about my other pains.

He shoved me away and reached for the next person.

I wasn't a person anymore. Just a number—161051.[1] I felt more lost than ever. My body shook as I tried not to let them see me sob.

Why did I jump under the couch? I thought. Why?

A man standing behind me put his hand on my shoulder.

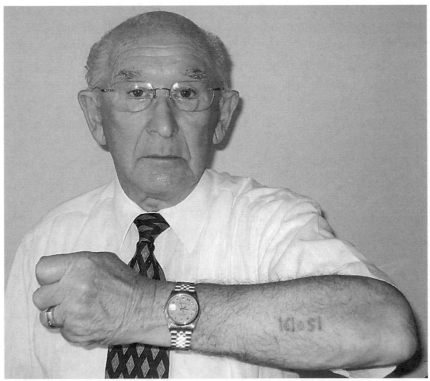

Photo by Anna Vaisman

DAVID FABER [photo 2005], showing the number 161051 that was tattooed on the outside of his left forearm at Auschwitz Concentration Camp, November 5, 1943 (Chapter 15 and References and Notes).

"Boy," he whispered. "Don't cry. There's nothing you can do. Just try to survive."

A guard stood by a pile of clothing with black and white stripes. He threw a jacket and pants at me, shoes with wooden soles, a strip of cloth with my number on it, a needle and a cotton thread. I put on the pants and shoes, both much too big for me.

Nobody told me what to do with the strip of cloth, but I looked at those who had been in front of me and saw it sewn on the front of their jackets. I did the same.

I went outside and stood with the others.

Trucks came, and guards yelled at us to get in. As I tried to pull myself up, one of them—young, with a blond mustache—pounded my back with a bat. Finally, two men reached down, took hold of my arms, and pulled me up.

My back hurt terribly. When I tried to stand up straight, it felt like a knife was stuck inside me. Some ribs must have been broken.

The trucks took us to a part of Auschwitz called Birkenau. There were huge, wooden barracks as far as I could see, forty or fifty. Inside each one was a single room almost filled with bunks three tiers high. Straw-filled sacks lay on them. In the center, the whole length of the building, was something like a long chimney, a kind of heater.

I wanted the top row, where it would be hard for the guards to hit me. Grunting with pain, I stood on the bottom row and pulled myself past the second level and onto the third. I collapsed, barely able to breathe, my back and chest hurt so badly.

The bunks weren't separate. Each level was one long bed where hundreds of men lay close to one another, one rough grey blanket for every five or six.

A barrack leader, a *Kapo*, stomped in and stood just inside the door.

"Listen!" he shouted. "My name is Potok, and I'll make you wish you'd never come here. You'll wish you'd never met me."

I wondered if he could be worse than the guards at Szebnia.

He walked along the bunks, grabbed the foot of a man in the middle row right under me, and yanked him onto the floor. No one spoke as the man lay sprawled on his stomach.

The *Kapo* bent over, his face close to the prisoner's.

"You look like you hid something," he said. "I'll bet you've got a fortune in your body. Give it to me!"

The man rolled onto his back, his hands held out palms up.

"No, sir." I could scarcely hear him. "I don't have anything, sir."

"You don't?"

The man spoke louder. "No, sir! Nothing!"

Potok smiled. "I'll find out."

He took a long, thin knife from a scabbard on his belt. "Give it to me, or I'll cut you open."

"Please don't!" The man tried to get up, but Potok pushed him down with his foot.

"Turn over!" he yelled and kicked the man in the head.

Crying, the prisoner turned to lie face down on the floor. Potok cut open the man's pants, then jabbed the knife into his anus and cut away pieces of flesh.

Screams rang through my head, and I covered my ears.

The screams stopped, and the *Kapo* laughed. "You know," he said, "he didn't have anything."

He pulled other people from the bunks, made them lie on their backs, and crushed their windpipes with his heavy boot. Then he would turn them over and butcher them the way he had the first man.

The rest of us lay in our bunks, some watching, some with eyes closed.

"Do you know what that smoke means?" a man wearing the Star of David asked as we stood outside the barracks the next day. He nodded toward a grey column rising from behind a high fence. "They're burning bodies. It goes on all the time."

"What do you mean?"

"They kill people with gas, and then they burn the bodies. Didn't you know that?"

"No," I said.

"Remember the trucks at the station, the ones with big tanks on the side?"

"Yes."

"Well, people who are too old or too sick to work are gassed in those trucks and then burned. That's what happens here, too, when you're no use to them anymore. Mengele comes every two weeks and makes a 'selection' for the gas chamber."

"Mengele?"

"*Dr.* Mengele.[2] You'll see the little bastard soon enough. Just pray you don't look worn out."

After months of starvation, I looked like a *Muselmann*, a word the Germans used to describe a starving person in India or the Middle East—nothing but skin and bones, half-dead, bones pushing against thin flesh, the will to live gone.

My time came on Mengele's third visit, as part of a long line of naked men and boys. Most were *Muselmänner*. One by one, we stopped in front of him as he sat erect on a straight, wooden chair. His cold, greenish eyes stared at each one of us, then more often than not he pointed to the number tattooed on a shrunken wrist. An assistant wrote it in a book, and the man was shoved toward a waiting truck.

But I hadn't given up; I wanted to survive. I had to show Mengele that I could work. Romek's words when we went to register, a lifetime ago, came back to me. "Stand up straight, look them in the eyes. Speak up!"

There was no chance to speak, but I stood up straight and stared at Mengele's eyes. The man ahead of me had slumped over and looked at the ground.

Mengele seemed surprised at my behavior. He hesitated, then pointed a finger at my number.

A guard pushed a rifle barrel against my back, and I stumbled away. More than a hundred from my barrack were picked for death that day and hauled off to the Birkenau crematorium. I was among them. Along the way, we passed a little orchestra, all women, playing Chopin's "Marche Militaire.".

We got down from the trucks, formed a single line outside the doors marked *Showers*, and waited. We knew we were there to die.

"I'm sorry, Mama," I whispered. "I tried."

I took the scrap of bread I had saved from my ration and put it into my mouth. There wasn't any reason to hoard it any longer.

A second fleet of trucks drove up and unloaded crowds of people. They were put into the line in front of us. Someone in the building pushed open the doors, and the line began to move into that terrible place.

With each step forward, my despair lessened. I had done my best to survive. Mama would understand.

The man ahead of me walked through the door, and I began to follow. Suddenly a guard thrust his rifle in front of me.

"The rest of you go back!" he ordered. "No more room!"

The door was pulled shut. I'd survived!

The fifty or so of us whose lives were spared this time walked to a truck. A woman stepped close to me, grabbed my hand, and squeezed it hard.

"You're going to live! She said. "I know it."

"Who are you?" I asked.

"Fania Fénelon."[3] She turned and walked away.

We climbed into a truck and went back to the barrack. I told myself over and over, I'm going to live, I'm going to live. I was sure more than luck had saved me. I remembered the old man in Tarnów after the massacre. He had told me, "God must want you to live." I'd keep on fighting to survive.

Trucks took us back to the barrack area. As I walked inside, the barrack leader was screaming and beating a prisoner with a piece of cable. I counted twenty-five blows.

The beating stopped, and the barrack leader turned to the rest of us.

"Everybody strip!" he shouted. "Go outside."

It was winter, probably February, with the temperature below freezing. We stood naked in the snow for about two hours. Almost all the older people died. Later I learned that we were being punished because someone stole a piece of bread from the barrack leader's room. He knew who did it, but he punished all of us.

Life in Birkenau had a pattern. New transports arrived; many persons were sent straight to the crematorium. My barrack filled again with the others. Soon Mengele would be back to sort out more *Muselmänner*, and another load would go to be gassed.

Transports came to Auschwitz day and night. The Nazis couldn't manage to gas them all, so they dug giant ditches. They put the men, women, and children in the ditches, poured gasoline over them, and burned them alive.[4] The screaming of these people I will never forget.

Many people gave up. We were allowed to walk outside the barrack once in a while, and each time I saw persons run to the fence and grab the charged wires, unable to endure more suffering and degradation.

Our toilet was another huge barrack with holes all over the floor.[5] There was almost no room to walk on the slippery boards, covered with frozen urine and feces. Sometimes people fell through a hole into the human manure. Every time I went there, I asked God to keep me from falling like that. It would be better to be shot than to die like that. I was so small, it would be easy to fall through.

Others were afraid, too. Some people urinated in their soup bowls rather than go to the toilet. The barrack leader found out and made us stand naked outside again.

There was a curfew every day at Auschwitz, at which time we were supposed to turn off all the lights. Sometimes the curfew was in the evening, and sometimes it was in the middle of the day. During a curfew, we were not allowed to leave the barracks, not even to use the toilet. I avoided the prospect of soup bowl by keeping a rag in my bunk, into which I would urinate if I was not able to go out to the latrine. Whenever I got a chance, I washed this rag with water, so I could use it again later if necessary.

Two weeks passed, and Mengele came back. Again, he sorted me out to go. This time, we went to a different crematorium, in the main part of Auschwitz. We were transported in the back of a dump truck that backed up to an open door. The front of the truck bed rose, and we slid into the crematorium.

But we slid into a hallway, not the gas chamber. A very high counter was on one side of the hall. I slipped under it and covered myself with the clothes piled there.

From my hiding place, I heard people screaming as the guards hit them with those big, wooden bats, forcing them into the gas chamber. I heard music from somewhere outside, and then a loud clang as the heavy, steel doors slid shut.

In the silence that followed, I peered out. Nobody was in sight. I sneaked from behind the counter and started toward the door that led outside. I had no idea where I would go. I just wanted to get out of there.

Someone grabbed my arm and jerked me around to face him.

"What are you doing here?" the Kapo demanded.

Down the hall, I saw men sorting clothes taken from the bodies after they were gassed.

"I got mixed up, sir," I told him. "I'm supposed to be down there sorting clothes."

"So what are you doing here? You're supposed to be with your *Sonderkommando*[6] group. Go back to your job."

"*Jawohl!*"

He pushed me toward the others. I was saved again.

I worked there for about three weeks, sorting clothes stripped from people who were gassed. Jackets in one pile, pants in another, shoes in a third. Then the man in charge stood with his hands on his hips.

"You *Schwein* have it too easy," he said. "It's time you did some real work!"

I was sent to sort inside the gas chamber itself. My job was to pull gold teeth from the mouths of the dead. The first few times I saw all the bodies—men, women, and children—I vomited. The sense of horror never left me, but after the first week I stopped throwing up.

A transport made up almost entirely of women and children came to the crematorium. When I went in, I saw a young woman, maybe around thirty, lying on the floor with an infant in her arms. The baby was alive, still nursing at its mother's breast.

I picked up the child, a beautiful little girl. Tears ran down my face as I held her in my arms and she looked up at me. I was wondering how I could save that baby. I knew there was a women's camp nearby. If I could smuggle the baby to the women, maybe they could save her.

"What are you doing with that baby?" a guard demanded.

"Nothing, sir. She was with her mother. I was bringing her

to you."

"You lying bastard Jew, you'll pay for that." He grabbed the baby and threw her into the fire.

He pulled out his revolver, jammed it into my back, and forced me ahead of him. We walked to the end of the camp near the barbed wire. There was a small building. He rang a bell. The door opened. He pushed me in, hitting me very hard.

Behind the desk was a Nazi officer. I looked at him, and I said, "I suppose this is the end of my life."

I recognized him. Many times I had handed him two cans of Zyklon B—a crystal poison the Nazis used for gassing prisoners to death—which he emptied out on top of the roof into the gas chamber below, making the poison gas.

He looked at me. He said, "You committed a crime, and I'm going to make you pay for it."

Photo by Richard Reck

At Auschwitz [2004] empty used cans of Zyklon B are preserved under glass.

Photo by Richard Reck

Pictured here [2004] is a small amount of the cans of Zyklon B that were used for gassing prisoners.

They tied me upside down to a big chair. One of the *Kapos* began to hit me with a rubber hose with a cable inside. I was supposed to count as he hit me, but I was in such agony that I lost my voice. Whenever I stopped counting, he kept starting over. He kept hitting me and hitting me.

Finally he stopped, and they untied me. As I lay on the floor, the officer stood over me and said, "It's too good for you to die. You'll wish I had killed you. You'll remember me until the moment you die. My name is Eichmann, Colonel Eichmann."

The following morning, a group of us was loaded onto a convoy of five or six trucks and sent off. I recognized part of the way. When I was very small, we used to go by car to this place quite close to Katowice. My mind filled with memories of those times, and I cried.

The truck made a sharp turn onto a gravel road and stopped in front of a high, wooden gate. Above it, I saw a sign like the one at Auschwitz, just a little different: *Arbeit macht das Leben frei*— Work Makes Life Free.

The gate swung open, and we passed through into another camp. I was at Jawiszowice, the coal mines. I had heard of Jawiszowice— the punishment camp.

CHAPTER SIXTEEN

Jawiszowice *The Punishment Camp*

I slid from the truck onto the snow-covered ground, shivering in the early-spring wind. A Gestapo officer pointed a gloved hand and shouted.

"You! You little one! Come here!"

I hurried to stand in front of him.

"Go down in the cellar over there. Push the boards out through that window. You hear me?"

"*Jawohl!*"

"Hurry up!"

He pointed to five other boys. "You go, too!"

The long boards were heavy, but I managed to drag one to the window and push it out. As I turned back for another one, I saw something lying on a pile of bricks. I picked it up and peered in the dim light. A pair of mittens!

Suddenly someone slapped me hard, and I staggered backward. Blood gushed from my nose, and my sight was blurred. I shook my head and wiped my face on my dirty sleeve.

"You stole my mittens!"

A man in prison clothes stood there glaring at me, his mouth in a straight line below a small moustache.

"Sir, I didn't steal your mittens. I just picked them up to see what they were. I come from a good home, and my parents taught me never to steal."

His look softened, and he took a clean rag from a pocket and wiped my face.

"I'm sorry," he said. "I didn't realize I hit a boy. Who are you? Did you just come into the camp?"

"Yes. My name is David Faber."

"Where did you live?"

"In Poland, in Katowice."

"Do you have any family left?"

"Only one sister. She went to Paris to the World's Fair before the war and never came home. Instead, she managed to get to England."

He folded the rag and put it back into his pocket.

"I used to live in Paris," he said. "Where did your sister stay? Did you have relatives there?"

"Yes. She stayed with our uncle Mila on rue du Temple."

"Mila Faber? I know that name. He owned tire factories."

He put his hand on my head, the first time anyone had touched me in friendship since Sammy died.

"You do come from a good family. I'm sorry I hit you." He smiled. "You must be hungry."

"Yes, I'm very hungry."

"My name is Paul. Paul Grachstein. I'm the camp electrician. I'll help you as much as I can. Come with me now, and I'll give you something to eat."

I began to cry. Paul put an arm around me and held me until I could say, "Thank you."

"Let's go," he said.

I followed him up wooden steps to a small room on the main floor of the barrack. Shelves with all sorts of electrical equipment lined the walls. Paul pushed aside one of them, and I saw a metal box behind it. He lifted the lid and took out a piece of bread and a glass jar of jam. With his spoon, he spread a thick layer of jam on the bread and handed it to me.

I hadn't seen jam since my brother and I hid in Judge Valah's secret room. I didn't know where he got it, and I didn't care. All that mattered was that I had a friend who cared what happened to me.

My hand trembled as I held the bread to my mouth and took a small bite. I chewed slowly to keep the taste and feel of food in my mouth as long as I could.

"Thank you, Paul," I said when the bread was gone and I had licked a smear of jam from my fingers. "Thank you very much."

He smiled and held out his hands, palms up.

"We have to help one another," he said. "Come every day, and I'll give you enough to keep you alive. And I'll try to keep you out of the mine. You'd die down there."

He patted my shoulder. "Now you'd better go before the guard misses you."

"Where did you go?" one of the boys demanded when I got back to the cellar.

"I had to go help the electrician do something," I said.

I couldn't tell them about the food, not if I wanted Paul to help me. He'd get into trouble, and I'd be as bad off as before.

"While we do all the hard work!" the boy said. "That's nice!"

I lifted the end of a board and dragged it to the window.

A few minutes later, a guard shouted from the top of the cellar steps. "*Appell! Appell!* Roll call! Roll call!"

We ran out into the big, open space surrounded by barracks. Men came from all sides, lining up in rows of five.

An SS man called out numbers, and I heard the prisoners answer all around me. "*Ja!*" "*Ja!*" I kept repeating 161051 in my mind, afraid I'd miss hearing it and be beaten for not answering. Finally it came, and I screamed, "*JA!*"

After that, I didn't think about anything except how cold I was and about the food I'd get from Paul tomorrow. The numbers stopped, and I heard a different voice.

"I am Colonel Heinrich Bischoff, the commander of this camp. I want you new prisoners who came in today to know that if you misbehave, you will be severely punished. This is Jawiszowice! This is the place where you end up dead unless you obey orders!"

He went on and on, the same threats I had heard before. I tried not to pay attention. After a long time he stopped, and I asked the man next to me, "Did he say anything?"

"We have to report to the barrack leader. He'll tell us the work we have to do and how to get fed."

I saw three boys standing together near the door as I came into the barrack. They looked about my age, and I thought how good it would be to have more friends.

"Hi," I said with a smile. "My name's David Faber. Would it be OK if I stuck with you fellows?"

One of the boys, tall with dark hair and eyes, looked at me. "Sure," he said. "Come on. My name is Jacob Banah."

"I'm Chaim Weiner, from Jaslo." The second boy was short with light-brown hair.

"I'm from Katowice," I said.

"Cracow," Jacob said.

The third boy spoke up. "My name's Janny, from Lvov. Maybe we can help each other if we stick together."

Another boy, even smaller than I, came up to our group.

"Hello," he said. "I'm Sammy Laufer. I don't know anybody here. Can I stick with you fellows?"

Chaim frowned. "There's four of us already. Maybe the *Kapo* won't like so many of us hanging together."

"Four or five, what difference does it make?" I said. "Let him come along."

Jacob and Janny agreed. The five of us found space together on the top row of bunks. I felt like I almost had a family.

Just before dark, loud military music came over the loudspeakers. I looked outside and saw a long line of men coming into camp. They looked worn out, their heads drooping forward, their arms hanging straight down. Coal dust smeared their faces and almost hid the white stripes on their prison clothes.

A man in one row slumped between two others, arms around their shoulders to keep him on his feet. If he fell, I knew the guards would shoot him or pull him out for the gas chamber.

That was what Paul wanted to save me from.

The five of us lay on the top bunk a little later, talking about our families before the war and trying to make our single blanket reach from one side to the other. I was lucky; I was in the middle, with someone on each side pushing close to stay warm. On the edges, Jacob and Chaim tugged the blanket first one way and then the other.

A loud voice broke into our talk.

"I'm the barrack leader, and you do exactly what I tell you! It's lights out, and I don't want to hear a sound! If I do, you'll wish I didn't!"

Nobody moved or said a word. Finally, I fell asleep. After what seemed like only minutes, the loudspeaker boomed again.

"Get up! The washroom's in the next barrack. You've got five minutes to clean up and get back!"

All around me, people jumped down from the bunks and rushed

to the washroom barrack. It was so crowded, I couldn't get near the water. I gave up and ran back unwashed, afraid I'd be beaten for being late.

I went to the back of a line going up to a big metal barrel. Someone touched my arm, and I turned to see Paul beside me. He bent over and spoke quietly.

"I've made the arrangements. As soon as you have your food, get away from this bunch. They're going to the coal mine. Come with me, and I'll put you in a line to work in a 'Shahkommando', a construction camp."

I nodded that I understood.

Near the front, a prisoner handed me an enamel bowl like the one in Birkenau. I dipped it into the barrel of weak coffee, and another prisoner gave me a small slice of bread, no more than two ounces at the most.

Paul waited while I drank the weak coffee and ate a bite of bread. Then he took me to a line of men by another barrack.

"I'll go with you," he said. "It's all arranged."

About a hundred of us went out of the camp and walked for more than an hour until we came to a wire gate with the sign "I. G. Farben."[1]

Inside, I followed Paul to meet the *Kapo*, Hans.

"This is David," Paul said, pointing to me. "He's a good boy. Try to take care of him."

"OK," Hans said. "I'll do what I can."

He gave me a pick and told me to work on digging a foundation trench that seemed to be endless. Part of it was finished, and men were putting in steel rods and building wooden forms for the concrete walls. I asked one of them what we were building.

"You saw the sign," he said. "Some kind of munitions factory."

A cold wind made my fingers stiff, and they hurt every time the pick struck the hard ground. Soon my back ached, and I had a pain in my side. I worked slowly, but I had to keep going. Anything was better than the coal mine.

Paul called to me after an hour or so.

"David, come with me. It's OK with Hans."

I set the pick in the trench, glad to be able to stop digging. Paul took me into a wooden hut that was the office for the construction job. A round, wood-burning stove with six rings on top sat on one side, a black stovepipe going up to a hole in the wall above it. A man, younger than Paul, sat at a small table beyond the stove. He looked up at us as we came inside.

"This is a friend of mine, Juziek Fuksenbruner," Paul said. "You'll stay with him and fix coffee for the workers."

The man said nothing, just frowned and stared at me.

Paul picked up a big can and handed it to me. "Fill this with water," he said, "and put it on the stove. When it boils, pour in this coffee."

The dark grounds looked like what Uncle Vanya made for the Russian partisans.

"That doesn't look like coffee," I said. "It looks like burned wheat."

"That's what it is. It's been baked." He laughed. "It's make-believe coffee. Go ahead and fix it. Let me know when it's ready. I'll send a boy to help you hand it out."

He left, and I did as he told me, grateful for the easy job and for the chance to be warm.

For a long time, Paul gave me extra food, and I had an easy job at the I. G. Farben site. I felt that I could survive if I kept out of the way of the barrack leader and the guards. But I wasn't sure I wanted to survive if the Germans won the war and this was the rest of my life.

Then everything changed. The *Lagerführer*, the camp leader, didn't like the way Paul did some wiring and locked him up for six weeks. I no longer had extra food, and without Paul's protection, I lost my good job. I went back to work on the construction job.

Sammy Laufer, the boy I had helped get into our group, got my job. I had introduced Sammy to *Kapo* Hans and asked the *Kapo* to help him if he could. Now Sammy made coffee in the warm hut, and I was outside, cold and hungry.

After a few days I asked him, "Sammy, could you give me some extra coffee or an extra piece of bread?"

He looked at me. "Who are you?" He sneered. "I don't know you. To hell with you!"

I never spoke to him again.

A boy about my age worked near me one day. I had seen him on the job before, but I didn't know his name. He broke his shovel handle trying to loosen the hard ground.

A guard ran up, yelling at him.

"You sabotaged German property." He hit the boy with his rifle butt.

That's what they said when anything broke. Then they'd kill the one who did it. I remembered Sammy in Szebnia.

The guards took the boy back to Jawiszowice and dropped him into a concrete-lined hole, seven or eight feet deep and about fourteen inches square. A wooden cover blocked all but a little bit of the top. He couldn't sit or turn around. Four days later, they pulled out his dead body.

The weeks passed. Paul was let out of jail and given his old job as camp electrician. He helped me again with extra bread, and I finally got back my job of fixing the coffee. I didn't know what happened to Sammy Laufer, and I didn't care.

Paul's electrical equipment and supplies were moved into the basement while he was locked up. It wasn't a real room, just a space in one corner, screened off by boxes of equipment. One day, I went down to see him and, without calling to him, pushed aside the canvas that hung over the entrance. Paul and his friend Juziek Fuksenbruner were listening to a radio!

Juziek saw me, pulled a revolver from under his coat, and pointed it at me.

Paul knocked the gun out of his hand.

"Are you crazy?" Paul demanded in a loud whisper. "That's David! Besides, they'd hear the shot."

"He knows," Juziek answered. "We can't let him live. It's too dangerous."

He bent down to pick up the revolver, but Paul pushed him aside and grabbed the gun.

"You aren't going to kill anybody." He glared at Juziek. "You can trust the boy. He didn't see what he saw. Don't worry. He's my responsibility."

I couldn't believe what I saw. A radio and a gun in the camp! I looked at Juziek.

"Don't worry," I said. "I'm alive because of Paul and you. Why would I say anything to the Germans? They killed my whole family."

He calmed down. "OK," he said, "but stay away from me."

"I didn't do anything to you, but I'll try to stay away. The first time I saw you I knew you didn't like me, but I don't know why."

I turned and went back upstairs.

We began to hear rumors that the Germans were losing the war. There were stories about the Russians pushing them back and about the allies landing in France. Still, nothing changed for us, and we didn't know what to believe. The Germans at the camp acted the same, as though we'd be there until we died, one way or another.

CHAPTER SEVENTEEN

Jawiszowice *Desperation and Hope*

A few weeks later, a transport of very young children arrived from Hungary. They were sent to the coal mine the next morning, and I was sent with them to be their interpreter. They spoke only Hungarian and Yiddish, so I told them in Yiddish what the *Kapo* said in German.

Paul went with us the first day and introduced me to *Kapo* Schmidt as he had to *Kapo* Hans earlier. He was a political prisoner, with a red triangle on his front pocket. When he saw how young the children were, he shook his head.

"Such little ones! I'll try to save them." He seemed to be thinking what he could do. "Come with me," he said. "I'll show you where you'll work."

I beckoned to the children, and we followed him over the rough, stone floor of the mine. A few of the children cried silently, but most seemed too tired and scared to do more than stumble along behind me.

Schmidt stopped by a long, moving belt that carried chunks of coal to the mine entrance.

"We have to get rid of the stones," he told me. "Put the children on each side, and they can pick out stones as they go by. It's the best job I can give them."

It was easy work for the older children, but not for the youngest, eight and nine years old. They couldn't lift the heaviest stones, and I tried to make sure the older boys or I picked out those. Everyone's hands bled from where ragged edges gouged and cut, and sometimes a stone dropped against a finger or a foot.

Kapo Schmidt never hit the children, never yelled at them. He gave us as much rest time as he could, but when the belt moved we had to work. If the coal wasn't cleaned of stones, Schmidt would be punished, and some new *Kapo* put in his place.

He and I became friends, and he told me why he was in

Jawiszowice.

"I'm a Christian," he said, "and I know the Nazis are wrong. I couldn't keep my mouth shut, so here I am."

I lay on my bunk one night, too tired to move. Someone was singing words I didn't understand. The song ended and began again. I thought the words might be Italian.

It began a third time, and I understood "mama." I raised my head and looked toward the singer. A small, dark-haired boy who had arrived the day before lay on his back nearby, singing in a sweet voice.

It was the first time I had heard anyone sing since Mother died. Tears came into my eyes as I remembered the lullabies she sang each night when I was small.

The boy stopped, and I called to him.

"What are you singing?"

He said something I couldn't understand.

"About your mama?" I asked.

"*Sì! Sì! Mamma!*"

He sat up and held his arms out, cradling a make-believe baby. He rocked from side to side a few times, then raised his arms as though the baby were nursing.

"Sing it again," I said and hummed a few notes I could remember.

He laughed and began the song again.

His name was Finci. We didn't speak each other's language, but we understood each other well enough through gestures and expressions. We seemed drawn to one another, and we soon learned enough words in common to be able to talk. He told me he was from Italy and that his family had been sent to different camps.

I switched places with Jacob so that Finci and I could be next to each other, and I soon learned the words of the lullaby the way I remembered he sang it:

	English translation:
Mamma, son tanto felice,	*Mama, I am happy*
perché ritorno da te.	*because I've come back to you*
La mia conzone mi dice	*my song tells me*
che il più bel fiore	*that the most beautiful flower*
è per te.	*is for you*
Mamma, solo per te	*Mama, only for you*
la mia conzone	*my song*
Vola.	*flies.*
Mamma, sarai con me tu	*Mama, you will be with me,*
non sarai più sola.	*you will never be alone*
Quanto ti voglio bene	*How much I love you*
queste parole d'amore	*this world of love*
che ti sospira il mio cuore	*comes from my heart*
forse non si usano più.	*maybe they don't use this any more.*
Mamma, la conzone mia	*Mama, my most beautiful song*
più bella sei tu.	*is you*
Sei tu la vita,	*you are the life*
ma per la vita	*but, for the life*
non ti lascerò mai più.	*I will never leave you again.*

In my job as interpreter, I could walk and mingle with the Polish miners who came from outside the camp every day. I became friendly with a lot of them, too. They had enough to eat but complained about how hard it was to get clothes. That gave me an idea.

Finci worked in the storage area, sorting clothes brought from Auschwitz and then sent out of the camp.

"Finci," I said to him one night as we ate our soup and bread, "I think I can get us extra food. But you'll have to help."

He looked puzzled.

"How? No food."

By this time, each of us knew the words for many ordinary things. I touched his jacket.

"You, shirt," I said, then lifted my jacket and pushed my hand up under it. "Bring here." I pointed to my bunk.

Suddenly he smiled. "*Sì! Bring shirt! Sì!*"

I pointed to my chest.

"I, shirt."

I pushed my hand under my jacket, pointed outside, and pretended to dig coal. I waved my hand as though I was telling someone to come to me, and then put my fingers to my mouth.

"Bread," I said.

Finci nodded that he understood.

"Men do?" he asked.

"*Ja*," I said. "Men do."

He frowned. "Germans shoot you, me."

"Be careful, not know."

"OK," he said.

When I came back from the mine the next day, I looked at Finci. He shook his head. "No," he said.

The next evening, he nodded as soon as he saw me. We climbed up to our bunks, and Finci pulled underwear and two shirts from beneath his jacket. I stuffed them under the blanket.

"Good," I said.

He grinned.

I wore the clothes under my striped uniform the next day and traded them to a miner for kielbasa and bread. Other workers wanted to do the same thing, and business was good for quite a while. Whatever I got, I shared with Finci and the others, Jacob, Janny, and Chaim. Sometimes it was a piece of margarine, sometimes cheese or kielbasa, most often bread. Thanks to Finci, we stayed alive.

"Guess who came in today," Jacob said when I got back from mine one evening. "An old friend from Auschwitz."

"A friend?" I frowned. "Who?"

"One of dear Potok's sweet brothers," Jacob said. "He got into some kind of trouble, and they sent him here to work in the mine."

"Isn't that nice." Janny grinned and rubbed his hands together.

The news spread through the camp, and by the next day everyone knew that a Potok was in Jawiszowice. And I heard the same words over and over. "He has to die."

Three days later, Potok didn't come back from the coal mine. Rumor said that he had been beaten to death, his body hidden somewhere.

The food from the miners and from Paul kept me alive, but by the middle of 1944 I was in a terrible shape. The work in the mine wasn't just hard, it meant almost no sunshine. I had one cold after another, and then the boils began to break out: two on my neck, one under my left arm, and an especially painful one in my groin. It hurt to move my head, and I almost screamed with every step. The colds got worse; I became feverish but still went each day to the mine.

Death would be a way out, I thought. But there was the promise to Mama. I couldn't throw myself against the electric fence, and I couldn't just give up. I had to stay alive, no matter how much I hurt.

The prisoners at Jawiszowice were given wooden shoes. The ones I wore rubbed my feet and gave me blisters that would bleed. I ripped pieces from my blanket to create makeshift mittens and socks by knitting them back together with my fingers. I had seen my mother knitting but had never before done it myself. I made the mitts and socks into square shapes. I still had boils, but there was an older man at the camp who told me about a cure: wet a piece of bread, even if it's just with saliva, then use it like a compress onto the affected area. The bread rations were very small, and I didn't have any. The man gave me his piece of bread, saying that he was old and would die soon anyway. I took a small piece of it and held it in my mouth as though it were hard candy. I followed the man's advice and managed to cure myself of all the boils except for the ones on my legs, which were very painful. Someone had a raw potato that I had tried to use on the boils, but that didn't help much. And I had to keep working or else end up in a crematorium. I got myself a rag by ripping a piece of a prisoner's suit from a dead body. I took the wetted bread from my mouth and put it on my boils, and wrapped the rag around it to hold the bread in place. The old man died a couple weeks later. He had been beaten to death because he couldn't run fast enough in those wooden shoes – shoes that rubbed against our feet so much that it was nearly impossible to walk.

I awoke before roll call one morning, feeling very sick. I'd have to do something. Maybe Paul could help me. I got up, almost fell, but managed to drag myself down the steps to the cellar.

I pushed aside the canvas over the entry to Paul's corner.

"Paul, help me."

He got up and came close to me.

"You look terrible, David. What is it?"

"I'm very sick. I can't make it to work today. I don't know what to do."

He put his hand on my forehead.

"You've got a high fever. You can't go to work. Go sign into the *Revier*."

That was the camp "hospital": one room, no doctor, no nurse. Nobody did anything for you, but you could rest there.

"All right," I said. "I'll go."

I started to fall, and Paul grabbed my arm.

"Can you get there by yourself?"

"I think so."

I reeled and fell against the barrack as I went outside. The *Revier* was two buildings away. I didn't know if I could walk that far. I should have let Paul help me.

I staggered up the steps and pushed open the door. A prisoner-clerk sat at a little table drinking coffee. He looked up at me, set down the cup, and let out a long breath.

"All right," he said.

I held out my arm. The clerk read my number—161051—and wrote it in the ledger in front of him.

"Take any bunk that's empty," he said and went back to his coffee.

There were a dozen bunks, all with people in them except for two on the top row and one at the end of the bottom row. I wanted the top. I had learned they didn't hit you as much up there.

I put a foot on the bottom bunk and tried to pull myself up. The boil under my arm felt like fire. I sucked in my breath, not moving for a few seconds. If I wanted to be on top, I'd have to stand the pain. Slowly, I climbed the rest of the way and collapsed on the bunk. I didn't want to make the clerk angry, so I closed my eyes and held my breath until it didn't hurt as much.

I lay there, feeling hotter and hotter. After what seemed like hours, I called to the man in charge.

"Please give me a drink of water."

He didn't answer.

I waited, then asked again.

He poured water from an enameled pitcher into a bowl like the one I used for food and brought it to me.

"Here," he said. "Don't spill it."

"Thank you."

The warm water soothed my throat a little. Half-asleep, I lay there the rest of the day.

I heard noises and opened my eyes. It was almost dark. Men were coming back from work. I heard them talking and their footsteps in the big room on the other side of the wall.

The door opened, and Paul stepped inside. As camp electrician, he could go anywhere. He carried a bowl of soup in one hand, bread and margarine in the other.

"Up here, Paul," I said.

He walked over and put his hand on my forehead. "You're still very feverish, son. How do you feel?"

"Not very well."

"Here, drink this soup. It's good for you."

He held the bowl to my mouth, and I swallowed. Then he broke off small pieces of bread and fed them to me.

"I'll see you tomorrow morning," he said when I had finished eating. "The colonel wants something fixed in his office tonight."

"Yes. Thanks for coming and for bringing the food."

I must have been completely exhausted, because I slept pretty well that night in spite of the boils and the fever. The work siren woke me in the morning. That meant it was a little after five. I heard men line up and go off to work.

I dozed for a while, then became wide awake. It seemed as though someone was trying to tell me something. Suddenly, I remembered what I had heard back at Auschwitz.

"You know, they don't need you sick," a man had said. "They

take you to the crematorium when you're no good to them."

My God, what am I doing? I thought. I've got to get out of here.

The clerk hadn't come in yet. Slowly, painfully, I got down from the bunk. I'd go to the toilet in the next barrack. Maybe it was only my fever and imagination that made me think they'd take me to the gas chamber. But I couldn't take the chance.

Soon I heard a noise and looked out the low window that ran along almost one whole side of the room. A truck drove up, one with a canvas cover and a big tank on the side. Two guards got out and went into the building. The driver backed to a few inches from the door. Then someone screamed, and figures moved across the narrow space between the *Revier* and the truck. The engine roared, and the truck moved away a little. A guard lifted the tailgate that reached halfway to the top, locked it, and climbed in.

If I had stayed on the bunk, I would be on the way to Auschwitz! What was I going to do? I was afraid to go back to my barrack. The clerk had written down my number. They'd look for me.

I hid in the hot, stinking toilet for hours, now and then peeking through the window to look for guards. About the middle of the day, I saw Paul and the clerk coming toward the *Revier*. The clerk said something and shrugged. Paul stopped, put his hands over his face, turned, and walked away.

Paul would know what to do. Maybe he could hide me somewhere. I slipped out a back door of the toilet and hurried after him. The boils felt like hot knives cutting my flesh, but I kept going.

I came close behind Paul and called his name.

He whirled around, eyes wide, mouth gaping.

"I don't believe it!" He pulled me to him, hugged and kissed me. "I don't believe it! How did you get away?"

I told him about remembering the man in Birkenau and about hiding in the toilet.

"God must have spared you," Paul said. "You're a son to me, and I felt like I'd killed you because I told you to go there. Thank God you escaped!"

"The clerk wrote down my number, Paul. They'll know I didn't get in the truck. They'll look for me."

"Don't worry," he said. "I'll take care of it."

Paul went back to the *Revier* and returned after a few minutes, with a piece of paper in one hand.

"Here," he said, "now you're safe."

It was a page torn from the clerk's ledger.

Paul smiled. They'll miss a lot of numbers, but they won't have yours."

Paul hid me in his room for several days until my fever went away and the boils were not as bad. He told *Kapo* Schmidt I was too sick to work in the mine and somehow arranged for me to go to another outside construction job. Paul knew that *Kapo*, too, and I didn't have to work hard for a while.

Our barrack *Kapo* was sent away to the other camp. He was a decent man and let us do pretty much as we wanted, as long as we didn't cause trouble. The new *Kapo*, Fritz, was another story.

Only five feet tall, he was broad, with powerful arms and hands, a devil who killed because it made him feel good. When he saw someone do anything he didn't like, he'd shout, "*Komm her!*"

The man would stand shaking in front of him, and Fritz would ask a question, any question. Before the man could answer, Fritz would make a fist with his left hand and act as though he were going to hit him. But he never did.

Instead, he'd drive the first two fingers of his right hand into the person's eyes. The man would fall to the floor and lie there screaming while Fritz beat him to death.

It had been a long time since I had believed in my father's God, the One who he said would take care of us. If He existed, that God had forgotten us or was punishing us for some terrible, unknown sins. It was better to depend on myself, to do whatever I could do to survive.

Only a few of the older men tried to observed Jewish rituals. Every Shabbat, they'd cover the scraps of bread with dirty rags, light the stubs of candle they had gotten somehow, bow their heads, and pray.

"Blessed art Thou, O Lord our God, King of the universe, who hast sanctified us by Thy commandments and commanded us to kindle the Sabbath lights.

"Blessed art Thou, O Lord our God, King of the universe, who bringest forth bread from the earth."

Quickly they'd snuff out the candles and eat the scanty food. The ritual seemed to give comfort to the old men, and I never made fun of them the way some of the younger Jews did.

Rumors of Russian victories and stories of great bombing raids on German cities came more often. They must be true, but nothing seemed to change for us.

One of the other boys I got to know well, Chaim Waksman, was a kleptomaniac. He had to steal things, whether he needed them or not. In late spring, Paul missed a pair of pliers with rubber grips and accused Chaim of taking them.

"I wouldn't steal from you, Paul," Chaim said. "And what would I do with your pliers, anyway?"

Two weeks later, we found out. The air raid siren sounded at about nine o'clock one night, and all lights went out. In the dark, Chaim used the pliers to cut a hole in the electric fence and escape. Weeks went by without any word of him, and we decided he was dead.

A new, exciting rumor ran through the camp. The Allies had landed in France and were pushing back the German army. We would be free before the winter! I wouldn't let myself believe it. It was too good to be true.

Late one afternoon in July, the siren wailed again.

"What's going on?" Jacob yelled. "Maybe the Russians are real close!"

I remembered my partisan friends and how good they had been to me. "That would be wonderful," I said. "They'd help us."

We heard an airplane engine and then the *chunk-chunk-chunk* of anti-aircraft guns. I looked out the window and saw papers floating down. The sky seemed full of them.

I couldn't bear not knowing what the papers said. I slipped out the side door of the barrack and picked up some that had blown against the steps. The guards in the towers couldn't shoot at me because the angle was too sharp.

The writing was in several languages—German, Polish, French, English.

"Hold on!" it said. "Don't give up! The Allies are very close. The Germans are losing the war."

I read the message and ran back into the barrack, waving the papers and yelling, "They're coming! They're going to get us out!"

People crowded around and grabbed the papers out of my hand.

"What are you talking about?" one old man demanded.

"Here, read it yourself!" I held out the paper. "The Allies are winning!"

He took the paper in a trembling hand and held it close to his eyes. After a moment, he dropped it onto the floor.

"Too late," he said. "Too late."

Finci looked out a window facing the camp fence.

"Come! Look!" he shouted.

I ran to the window. The highway to Katowice ran along the other side of the fence. Two German soldiers, rifles leveled in front of them walked down it, behind a man wearing a leather jacket with an American flag on the shoulder. He looked toward the barracks and waved one hand above his head.

"They *are* coming, Finci!" I grabbed his arms and shouted again. "They didn't forget us! They're coming!"

"*Si!*" Finci laughed and clapped his hands. "*Si*, they come!"

In the morning, everything was the same, but I felt different. I knew what the leaflets said was true. There was hope of freedom. Please, God, soon.

After the leaflets were dropped, the *Kapos* were forbidden to strike the prisoners. Fritz was moved from our barrack, and things became easier. The leaflets were right, I thought. Freedom is coming!

Then one morning in late September, the loudspeakers blared, "*Appell! Appell!*"

We ran into the center of the camp and lined up in front of the scaffold that stood there. There were whispers about the Russians being only a few miles away, that we were going to be sent to another camp, and even that the Germans were going to let us go.

None of it was true. Chaim Waksman was half-thrown out of a truck, his hands tied behind him. A guard pushed him toward the scaffold and up its three steps.

Colonel Bischoff stood on his little platform and shouted, "This man escaped and will be punished by hanging. Anyone else who tries it will get the same!"

So much for the rumors. Bischoff stopped talking. Chaim lifted his head and shouted. *"Haverim!* Friends! David! Jacob! Janny! They're coming! Americans, British, Russians. I'm the last one to die! You're going to live!"

Seconds later, they hanged him. But he died with dignity.

For the next two months, I didn't work. I just stayed in the barrack. Without the food from the miners, all of us suffered. We weren't beaten anymore, and we heard more rumors about the Russians coming, but the hope we'd had from the leaflets and from Chaim's words faded. I didn't know how I'd live through another winter.

Many of the *Kapos* were criminals convicted of murder and other serious crimes, or they were political prisoners. The camp commander ordered us to clean an empty barrack, and then he brought in prostitutes. For three days and three nights, *Kapos* went in and out of that barrack.

CHAPTER EIGHTEEN

DEATH MARCH *One Step at a Time*

In late November or early December 1944, we had another five a.m. roll call. But this time it was different. We came out into the freezing morning to see regular soldiers. Wehrmacht, standing all around the edges of the big, open space. Some had rifles; many held machine guns.

I turned to Jacob standing next to me.

"Something's going to happen, Jacob. I'm scared."

"Yes," he said. "We've never had real soldiers before. And look at all those trucks outside."

I looked through the fence. A long line of trucks stretched down both sides of the wide road as far as I could see. Soldiers leaned against the cabs or stood in groups of two or three. Regular soldiers, not the SS troops that always were in the camps.

"Maybe they're going to haul us back to Auschwitz," I said. "To the gas chambers."

The camp leader, Colonel Bischoff, came out of his office and climbed onto the little platform he used when he made a speech.

His first words were, "The High Command has ordered this camp closed."

I couldn't believe I'd heard him right. They never told us anything. All they did was give orders and make threats.

"Chaim must have been right," I said. "The Russians or somebody are close, and the Nazis don't want us to get free."

"You're going to another camp," Bischoff went on. "Anybody who tries to escape will be shot. Take your blanket. Leave everything else behind."

He stomped down the three steps and went back into his office.

Leave everything else behind? All I had was a bowl, a striped suit, and that heavy blanket with Russian words woven into one end of it. That's all anybody had.

"Hey, David," Jacob said. "How do you like leaving everything behind? That'll break my heart."

"Sure," I said. "It's a shame to leave it all here."

We were cold and hungry, but we laughed.

We stood outside almost all day. In late afternoon, the *Kapo* sent us back into the barrack, where we got a little coffee and a double ration of bread. A double ration! Maybe things were going to get better. Or maybe it was some kind of trick.

After almost two years in that camp, I knew how to survive. Now it was changing. We'd go somewhere new, and I'd have to learn all over again—maybe in a place like Auschwitz. And nobody knew when we'd get more food. I tore off a small piece of bread and held it in my mouth before I swallowed it. I put the rest in my pocket.

"Get your blankets and go outside," the *Kapo* yelled as soon as the bread was handed out.

I pulled the thick blanket over my shoulders and hurried out into falling snow.

The gates were open, and we walked out to the road. But the trucks had gone. I wondered why they'd been there. Somebody must have changed the plan.

I gripped the blanket, holding it close under my chin. Thank God for it! It was so big I'd unraveled long threads, and with sticks for needles, knit socks and gloves. I had learned to knit by watching my mother do it when I was a little boy. I'd shown Finci and the other boys how to do it.

We moved away from the floodlights of the camp, slipping and stumbling in the fresh snow. Jacob and Finci were on one side of me, Janny on the other. Paul and Juziek Fuksenbruner were in the row just ahead.

Paul and Juziek looked like babushkas,[1] with scarves over their heads. Before we left the lights, I noticed they also had earphones. Each of them had a little box in one hand, and I heard a tapping noise, like Morse code. *Bup—bup, bup—bup, bup—bup*, it went on for quite a while.

We'd gone only a little way before Jacob started complaining.

"My feet hurt," he said. "I can't see where I'm going, and I'll fall in these damned wooden shoes."

"Shut up!" Janny said. "Everybody's feet hurt. I'm tired of your complaining."

"At least your feet are warm," I said. "You're not like most people, who don't have socks."

"Or gloves," Janny added.

I was talking to Jacob and Finci and trying to keep the blanket tight around me. Suddenly I noticed that Paul and Juziek weren't in front of me anymore.

"Where'd they go?" It was snowing harder now, and I couldn't see more than a few feet. "They were here just a minute ago."

"Well, they're gone now," Jacob said. "I hope they get away."

I wasn't sure how I felt: glad that Paul had escaped, afraid he'd be shot. Maybe they had sent signals to people who would help them. I didn't care what happened to Juziek, but I wanted Paul to live.

And I was jealous, too. Paul had told me I was like a son to him. Now he'd escaped with Juziek. Maybe he didn't care for me as much as I'd thought. But I needed him, and I'd miss him.

Maybe I wouldn't need him anymore. Nobody knew where we were going. Maybe I'd die before we got to the other camp. Maybe they'd kill us when we got there. So who cared about Paul?

We went on all night, dragging our feet as the snow got deeper and deeper. The weakest people, the sickest ones, began to stumble. Some were helped by persons near them; many fell and lay in the snow. Those who couldn't go on were shot. The Germans never left anybody alive behind.

Hours passed, and the shots came more often. A man in the row behind me fell against my back. I turned and saw him sprawled on his stomach. A guard raised his rifle and shot. The rows behind him stepped over his body, and we went on.

We stopped before daylight. It felt earlier than the usual five o'clock roll call, and it looked darker.

"Sit down!" the guards yelled.

I took off my blanket, put one end in the snow, and pulled the rest back around me. It was easy to think about giving up. But I knew I wouldn't. I'd fought too hard to stay alive. There might still be hope. Maybe the Allies, whoever they were, would manage to free us before too long. I curled up on my side and went to sleep.

"Get up! *Schweine!* Get up!"

I opened my eyes and sat up. Guards ran along the road, yelling and poking at people with their rifles. Jacob was already standing, rubbing his gloved hands over his face. I got to my feet.

Finci lay wrapped in his blanket.

I put my foot against his back and pushed. "Get up, Finci! Quick! The guard's coming."

He rolled over and got up, mumbling something in Italian.

People coughed and spit, stamped their feet in the snow. Others urinated where they stood. Like animals, I thought. That's what the Nazis were making us. Animals.

Some didn't get up, not even when the guards kicked them.

I looked toward the front but couldn't see the end of the line. It was the same in the other direction. There were hundreds and hundreds of people.

"How can there be so many people?" I said. "I know a lot died last night, but it looks like more than when we started."

Jacob looked both ways. There were people as far as we could see.

"You're right," he said. "Some other camp must have joined us last night. Maybe Auschwitz."

The guards shouted at us to get into rows of five. Slowly the line began to move again. The snow had stopped, but grey clouds hid the sun, and a cold wind blew in our faces. The snow on the road was packed down by the people in front of us, and it was easier to walk. Still, we heard shots in front and back of us and passed bodies lying where they fell.

I looked at the ground, forcing myself to keep going, one step at a time. At about noon, the sun came out as we stopped again. They gave us nothing to eat or drink. That's why we got a double ration of bread the day before. I had saved most of mine, and so had Jacob and Finci. I had talked them into doing that a long time ago.

"Eat a little bit at a time," I told them. "Always make sure to save some for later. It's not so hard that way. It makes you feel better to know you have something left."

I didn't know why, but they usually listened to me.

Each of us took out the bread we'd wrapped in rags torn from a prison uniform, and broke off a little bite. Too tired to talk, we sat on our blankets by the edge of the road. The snow was deep there and clean underneath the top. We put handfuls of it into our mouths a little at a time. There was nothing else to drink.

We moved on, feet sore, bodies aching. A boy I didn't know walked next to me, on my right. I asked his name.

"David," he said. "David Michaelman."

"Mine's David, too. David Faber."

I was surprised when he told me he was sixteen, almost seventeen. He looked older than I.

"I'm older than you," I said. "Eighteen. What about your family?"

"I have two brothers and three sisters. The Nazis came in one day and took them all. I was little and hid behind a cabinet. Sometimes I wish they'd found me."

"I know," I said. "My family was all killed, except for one sister in England. My parents, five sisters, and one brother. A lot of times I think I'd be better off if I'd died with them."

He went on. "My father was a religious man, went to synagogue every morning. I loved him very much. Everybody did. He told me stories and made me laugh a lot. I don't know what happened to him. To any of them."

"My father was very religious, too. My mother took care of the business. He mostly went to the synagogue and read books. But he was good to us, and we all loved him."

Just before dark, we stopped a little way past a house and barn. Again, we had nothing to eat or drink except a bit of the bread and more snow. I heard cows lowing in the barn and thought how good milk would taste. But there wasn't any way to get in. Guards were everywhere.

I lay there by the side of the road, thinking about the cows and the milk. Finally, I said to David, "Milk would taste wonderful. Let's sneak over to the barn and get some."

"No," he said. "I don't want to get shot."

"How about you, Jacob?"

"I'll go," he said. "Hell, I don't care if they shoot me. There's nothing to live for."

I asked Finci, too.

"No, not safe," he said. "Moon bright. Soldiers see."

"Well, we're going," I said. "The soldiers are all asleep. Watch our blankets, you fellows. Come on, Jacob."

We crawled slowly, staying as low as we could. Our hands sank into the soft snow, and the front of our clothes soon got wet. When we were a good way from the road, we got up and ran to the barn.

"Wait," I whispered. "Don't open the door yet. See if you can hear anybody first."

We stood there, listening.

"I don't hear anything," Jacob said. "Let's go in."

The door creaked when Jacob pulled it open enough for us to slip inside. Four cows stood in the shadows cast by the moonlight coming through a high window. They turned their heads and stared at us with their big, soft eyes, their warm breath making white puffs.

"Look at them, Jacob," I said. "We're going to get some milk."

"Maybe it's all gone," he said. "I don't know how to milk a cow, anyway. Do you?"

"No."

"And we've got nothing to put it in."

We looked around but couldn't see anything.

"Well, I'm going to get some," I said.

I lay down on my back and slid my head under the cow. She paid no attention, just kept chewing.

"What are you doing?" Jacob said. The cow will step right on your face."

"Nah, she doesn't care. But I can't milk her like this." I touched the cow's teat. "Take hold of these and squirt some milk into my mouth."

He shrugged. "I'll try." He knelt by the cow, put his hand around one of her teats, and squeezed. No milk came out.

"You've got to squeeze from the top," I said. "I know that much."

"Well, why don't you show me if you know how?" He sounded mad. "Maybe the farmer got it all."

"You can do it, Jacob. Keep trying."

The cow's tail slapped the back of Jacob's head.

"Damn it," he said. "She's getting mad."

"She's OK. Just try again."

"All right. But just one more time."

He took hold of the teat, and this time he must have done it right because warm milk squirted into my face.

"It's coming," I said. "But you have to aim better."

The second squirt went right into my mouth. I choked and thought I'd die before I could stop coughing.

Jacob yanked me from under the cow and sat me up. Then he pounded my back. Milk sprayed out of my mouth.

"Got any other great ideas?" he asked when I finally could breathe.

I shook my head, still not able to talk.

Jacob got up and walked toward the other end of the barn. Soon he came back, holding up a tin bucket.

I found this on a pile of straw," he said. "You try this time."

"OK."

I'd never milked a cow, either, but I could do it if Jacob could. We took turns squeezing and pulling. The cow could tell we didn't know how to do it. She kept hitting us with her tail and lifting her hind leg as though she wanted to kick us.

We got about half a bucket of milk before it stopped coming. I lifted it to my mouth and took a long drink.

"God, that's good," I said. I wiped my mouth. "Here, have some."

Jacob took the bucket and drank, then handed it to me.

There was some left after we'd drunk all we could hold.

"Can we take this back to the other guys?" Jacob asked.

"We can't crawl and carry a bucket," I told him. We'd spill it. They should've come along."

We walked partway to the road, then dropped to our hands and knees. The guards were still asleep and didn't see us.

Janny opened his eyes as I crawled up beside him.

"We drank a lot of milk, Janny," I told him. "It tasted wonderful. There's some left in a bucket. Why don't you go drink it?"

"No," he said. "I've gone through hell all these years and

survived. I'm not taking chances just for milk."

"OK, but it's sure good."

I crawled under the blanket I shared with another boy named Klaus. Jacob and Janny slept in the same way, one blanket under them and one on top. It was warmer than sleeping alone.

Klaus rolled over and pulled the blanket off me. I pulled it back until I was covered. We kept doing that until I fell asleep.

It seemed only a few minutes before the guards shouted at us to get up, and I opened my eyes. The sun wasn't up yet, but it was getting light.

I got up right away, before a guard could hit me with his rifle. Klaus lay still.

"Get up, Klaus," I said. "You want to get hurt?" I reached down and shook him. He didn't move. I slapped his face. "Come on! Get up! The guard's coming!"

I pulled the blanket away from his head and shoulders. His face looked as white as the clean snow. He couldn't get up. He'd frozen to death.

I picked up his blanket.

CHAPTER NINETEEN

BUCHENWALD *What Else Could Happen?*

We plodded on, stopping only a few minutes at noon to eat the last of our bread. Then on again, barely lifting our feet, just trying to keep moving. Most of the time the only sound was snow creaking under our wooden shoes. Once I slipped and fell to my knees.

"Get up!" Finci yelled. "They'll shoot!"

He grabbed my arm and pulled.

"I'm OK," I said. "I just slipped."

"It's almost dark," Jacob said. "Why don't we stop? I can't stay on my feet much longer."

"Bastards!" Finci said. "Don't give a damn."

Finally, well after dark, the guards shouted at us to stop. I spread Klaus' blanket at the edge of the field and dropped onto it. Finci and Jacob lay down, one on each side of me, and we covered ourselves with the rest of the blankets. There was nothing to eat, but maybe we would be warm enough to sleep.

I heard a faint noise, like engines. I raised my head and poked Jacob. "Listen!"

The Germans heard it, too, and ran into the field. They didn't shout at us. They just ran. Before we could get up, the planes were over us, bullets pouring onto the crowded road. In the glare of their lights, I saw people scramble up and start to run into the dark. Bodies jerked as bullets hit, and they fell, sometimes on top of one another.

"My God!" Jacob shouted. "They think we're Germans!"

Even our friends were killing us.

We ran into the field. After a few minutes, the planes came back. I tried to dig into the snow, somehow thinking I'd be harder to see lying flat on my stomach.

Three times the planes flew over and shot at us. Each time their lights showed more people on the ground, killed or wounded. It didn't matter which. The Germans would shoot anybody who couldn't go on.

The guards shouted at us to get back on the road and lie down.

We found our blankets still spread on the snow and lay down again. From all around, we heard groans and calls for help. There was nothing to do except try to stay warm.

Before daybreak, the Germans got up those who were alive, and we went on. I could see the ends of the line now, so many had died in the cold or from the bullets the night before. Frozen bodies lay everywhere. Blood put new stains on the dirty snow.

Just before dark, we got to a railroad station. A train with empty cattle cars stood waiting.

"Maybe we're going to ride," I said.

"I hope so," Jacob said. "I'm damned tired of walking."

The guards yelled at us to get onto the train.

"You lucky bastards!" one near us said. "Your own special train."

Snow had blown into the cars, leaving only small bits of the floor uncovered. Cow manure lay thick in the bare spots and must have been under all the snow. Not many of us were still alive, so there was plenty of room. Only a couple of dozen people were in the car with me. I sat in a corner on Klaus's folded blanket, wrapped mine around me, and leaned against the sides of the car. The other boys huddled close to me.

It began to snow again before we left the station. Big flakes covered everything. Every few minutes, I brushed them off my face and blew them from my lips.

The train rattled through the dark for several hours, sometimes whistling and slowing for a station, then picking up speed again.

I saw a sign that read *Huchenbach* and then the words *Buchenwald Lager*.

The train moved ahead slowly and stopped by a platform like the one at Auschwitz. What happened next was like Auschwitz, too. SS men unfastened the heavy locks and slid open doors. Then the yelling began.

"Out, you pigs! Get out!"

I grabbed one of the boards on the side and pulled myself up. The guards would come in after us if we didn't hurry. We jumped out onto the platform, where the *Kapos* swung wooden bats and rubber hoses at anyone they could reach.

"Five!" they shouted. "Rows of five!"

It was always five. We did it without thinking.

The *Kapos* walked between the rows, writing down numbers as we held out our arms. Then, for hours, we waited. We had nothing to eat or drink.

I had decided long before that making us stand and wait was part of their scheme to punish us. They always did it. Finally, they yelled at us to move off the platform, and we marched to a barrack.

The *Kapo* began to assign sleeping places, but we didn't pay any attention.

"Jacob! Finci!" I said. "Take the top! Hurry!"

We scrambled up to the third row. I dropped Klaus's blanket onto the bare boards.

"Let's lie on this one and pull all the others over us," I said.

We huddled close together under the three blankets and had just begun to feel warmer when the *Kapo* yelled at us to line up outside again.

This time we got a piece of bread and what was supposed to be coffee. The dry bread tasted like shopped-up straw. But it was something in our stomachs, something to help us survive.

I wondered when the Allies would get there. Surely they were coming soon.

The next day we were in quarantine, waiting for assignments to jobs. We lay on the bunk for a while, then Finci said, "Good outside. Sun warm."

Jacob and I agreed, and we stayed outside for hours, moving with the sun. In late afternoon, the *Kapo* ordered us back inside.

"You filthy animals," he said. "You're going to have a bath."

We went to another barrack, a huge building with an enormous, indoor pool. The water in it looked different, light-green instead of clear.

"Strip and jump in!" the *Kapo* ordered.

As soon as the first people slid into the pool they started screaming. The rest of us hung back, but the *Kapos* hit us with bats and hoses, and the SS men hit us with their rifles and drove us into the pool.

I remembered something I'd learned from Papa when I was a little boy. People didn't have showers then. Instead, we'd go each week to an indoor pool where we'd strip and duck ourselves a few times. I didn't like it because water got into my ears and nose. Papa used to tell me at mikvah,[1] "David, do what I do. Plug your ears. Push against your nose with your middle fingers. Keep your mouth closed. Duck yourself three times. This is God's wish, that you come out clean for Shabbat."

I remembered, and yelled to Jacob and Finci.

"Put your fingers in your ears! Hold your nose! Keep your mouth shut! And your eyes!"

People climbed out of the pool screaming and crying. Many others floated in the water or lay on the bottom.

The SS men pushed us into the pool. It didn't feel like water. It burned. I grabbed for the side and pulled myself out.

Jacob climbed out after me. Finci must have been mixed up with his eyes closed. He started to move away from the side of the pool, toward the middle.

"Finci!" I yelled. "Finci! Stop! We'll help you out!"

He stopped and held up his arms. Jacob and I reached down and pulled him out.

Showers lined the walls. Each of us got under one and let the cold water pour over us. I squinted at Jacob and the other people. Then I looked at my own body.

All my hair was gone. My armpits and my groin burned like they were on fire. Blisters covered my body, as if somebody had poured boiling water over me. My lips were swollen. My eyes were almost closed.

I picked up my prison uniform, but I couldn't stand to have it touch me. My skin was peeling. Naked, I went outside. The cold felt good on my burning skin. After a few minutes, the *Kapo* ordered us to go back to our barrack.

On the way, I picked up snow and touched it to my body. I washed a dirty rag, filled it with snow, and patted the places that burned the most. My back hurt terribly.

"Finci, put some snow on my back, please," I said.

He filled his soup bowl, dipped his fingers in it, and held them very gently against my back.

"Oooh, that feels good," I said. "I'll do it for you." The *Kapo* yelled for us to put on our clothes and get into the barrack. We helped one another slip on our jackets, and then each of us slowly, carefully, pulled on our pants and limped inside.

"How the hell can I get up to the top?" Jacob said. "I can't hold on to anything."

"Well," I said, "it'll be worse if they hit us. We can't stay down here."

Finci reached up and slowly put his fingers around a board. He drew in a sharp breath but said nothing. He put one foot on the bottom bunk and pulled himself up, then crawled the rest of the way. I saw blood smeared on the boards.

"Go on, Jacob," I urged.

"If Finci can do it, I can," he said. "But I'll do it faster. Get it over with."

He grabbed hold of a board and screamed. "Ayeee!" But he kept going all the way to the top.

I followed, going slowly the way Finci had. The boards tore my flesh, and I left my own bloodstains.

We had to put the blankets over us to keep from freezing, but they felt like a million needles jabbing into our raw flesh. We lay there all night, falling asleep for a few minutes, then waking whenever one of us touched another.

The Germans left us alone for two weeks, and the pain gradually decreased. It still hurt when anyone touched me or if I bumped into anything, but my clothes didn't rub raw flesh anymore.

I wondered what else could happen. How much more could they do without killing us? It was hard to keep hoping to get free, but I had to believe that I would. The Germans were losing the war, I was sure.

Finci walked into the barrack and called to me.

"Hey, David, come, go outside. Nice in sun."

"OK."

I joined him, and we walked down the road toward the main gate. Many new prisoners were coming into the camp.

"Look," Finci said, "new transport. Let's see what people come in."

"OK. Maybe we'll see somebody we know."

We walked closer. Suddenly Finci yelled.

"David, look!"

He grabbed my arm, and I screamed.

"Finci! You're touching me! It hurts!"

He let go and pointed toward the new prisoners.

"Look! My *papà*!"

"You're imagining things."

"No! My *papà*! I know!"

He started off, and I grabbed the back of his jacket.

"Finci! Don't go!" I screamed at him. "Don't go!"

He struggled to get away, pulling so hard the button ripped off his jacket. I couldn't hold him back.

"*Papà! Papà!*" he shouted as he ran to his father. The man looked up, his mouth dropped open, and he stepped out of the line. Finci reached him, jumped into his outstretched arms, and kissed him over and over. His father lifted Finci off the ground and held him tightly. I was close enough to hear, "Finci! Finci! Finci!"

Jacob ran up to me.

"What's Finci doing?"

"He found his papa," I told him. "I can't believe they're so lucky. It's a miracle."

"Yeah."

I thought of my own father, beaten to death long before. Maybe he was better off. He might have starved or been gassed. Nobody would know. At least his family had grieved for him.

A minute later, a tall SS man elbowed his way through the crowd.

"*Was ist los?*" he demanded. "What is going on?"

A prisoner turned and said in German, "The boy found his father."

"He *what*?"

"He found his father. They're lucky people."

"That's not lucky."

That Nazi took his revolver from a side holster and shot Finci's father in the head.

Finci stood there, staring at his father on the ground, blood oozing from his head. He didn't make a sound. Then he looked at the German. You could see how he hated him.

The SS man glared back at Finci, and I was afraid he'd shoot him, too. Instead, he put away his gun and walked off.

Finci made a loud noise and fell on top of his father's body, sobbing.

Some men brought a two-wheeled cart and pulled Finci away. They picked up the body and dropped it onto the cart. Finci ran alongside as they moved away. He picked up his father's hand and held it against his chest.

"*Papà mio, Papà mio*," he said over and over.

A *Kapo* grabbed him. "Where do you think you're going?"

Finci jerked away, still holding his father's hand.

"No, Finci," I shouted. "No!" Jacob and I tried to pull him away from the cart. "Finci, don't! Don't give up! Please, Finci, come with us!"

We held his arms and took him back to the barrack.

CHAPTER TWENTY

DORA-MITTELBAU *Tunnels*

The *Kapo* woke us before daylight two days later. It was the same thing I'd been through so many times. We hurried outside; they called our numbers; we waited until almost dark. Then trucks drove up. SS men and *Kapos* surrounded us, beating us and yelling.

"Run! Into the trucks! Run!"

I always had trouble getting into the high trucks. This time I hit my knee against the metal edge of the bed and fell back onto the ground. A guard kicked me with his heavy boot and yelled at me to get up.

I struggled to my feet, and two middle-aged men lifted me into the truck. I limped to the side and leaned against the canvas. One of the men pushed up my pants leg and looked at my bloody knee. He took a rag from his pocket, wrapped it around my knee, and tied it tightly.

"Take it easy, boy," he said. "You'll be all right."

"First chance you have, wash that rag," the other man told me. "You've got to keep the cut clean."

"I'll try," I said. "Thanks."

"I had a son," he said. "He'd be about your age, I guess. I don't know if he's alive or dead."

"Where are you from?" I asked.

"Cracow," the first man told me.

"I'm from Sosnowiec," the second man said. "Near Silesia."

"I was in Sosnowiec for a little while," I said. "Then we moved to Tarnów."

"Does anybody know where we're going?" the first man asked.

Nobody answered for a moment. Then someone nearby said, "What difference does it make? They'll either kill us or make us work like dogs."

Late that night, we saw floodlights ahead of us. As we got closer, I read the sign *Mittelbau Lager Dora*.

The gates opened, and the long line of trucks drove in. Each one turned and backed against a long, concrete platform. Chains rattled as guards loosened them and let down the doors. *Kapos* and SS men were all around.

They yelled at us, "Get into line! Stand up straight!" They hit us with bats and hoses. German shepherd dogs snarled and bit. It reminded me of Auschwitz, and I felt like I was having the same nightmare over and over.

I didn't know where Jacob and Janny were, but I hoped they were nearby. Finci hadn't come with us. He was put in a different group.

An SS sergeant called our numbers and sent us to different groups along the left side of the platform. We waited there until almost daylight, then marched off to a big barrack like the ones at Auschwitz.

My knee was swollen and hurt terribly, but I forced myself to climb to the top row. I knew it was better to be up there. We had to leave our blankets at Buchenwald, and now there was only one for every two people. They were big, and seven of us lay very close together, with one blanket underneath and two covering us. That way we kept from freezing.

We had nothing to eat or drink until very late in the evening, not even water. Then we stood in line for a slice of bread and soup so thin that it was impossible to tell what it was supposed to be.

I finished my soup and, as always, I saved a tiny bit of bread rolled into a rag. Before going to sleep, I put it between my legs so nobody could steal it.

Kapos came in the next morning.

"Up, you filthy bastards!" they yelled. "You dirty garbage! Get up!"

We hurried out into the big square surrounded by barracks, like Auschwitz. Soon they called out our numbers and put us into different work groups.

We ran through the open gate to where trucks waited to haul us somewhere. Guards with rifles and dogs ran alongside every other row. A man in front of me slipped and fell. People behind him tripped and piled on top. SS men kicked them, and dogs bit their legs and they struggled to get up.

The trucks climbed up a winding road through thick forests. It got steeper and steeper and finally ended near high mountains. The trucks stopped, and guards began yelling at us to get out.

I jumped onto the rocky ground, wondering why they had brought us to this place. I couldn't see anything but forest, except for a wide trail that went up from the end of the road.

"Line up!"

When we got into rows of five, the guards ordered us to go up the trail. It was hard to walk without stumbling on loose rocks. My throat and lungs burned as I sucked in cold air. The trail twisted between the trees for a mile or so before we stopped by what looked like toy train tracks.

They came around the base of the mountain and went straight into a hole cut out of the rock in front of us. Four-wheeled carts rattled and scraped against the rails as men pushed them into the opening. All the carts were empty, and I wondered why six men were with each one.

I soon found out.

A *Kapo* pulled six of us out of line.

"Bring that!" he yelled and pointed to an empty cart. "Follow me!"

We took hold of the cart and pushed it into a tunnel cut out of solid rock. As we stepped inside, the roar of jackhammers poured over us, drowning the sounds of the wheels against the tracks. In the dim light from the bulbs along the walls, I could see more tunnels branching off on either side. We went straight ahead, deep into the mountain and finally turned into one of them.

The noise got louder, the dust thicker. At the end of the tunnel, men were drilling into the rock face, knocking off chunks of stone. Other men loaded the chunks into the little carts and pushed them away through another tunnel going off to the left. The *Kapo* pointed to the stones on the tunnel floor. That was our new job.

I picked up a big chunk, and the rough edges cut into my skin. I dropped it into the cart and pressed my hands against my back.

"Pick up the rocks!" A *Kapo* hit my shoulder with a bat. "Get to work!"

I bent over and picked up another piece.

We pushed the loaded cart out of the mountain and on to a

place where the earth dropped away for hundreds of feet. Two men pulled a lever that tilted the cart, and the stones rumbled down the steep cliff. Then we pushed the cart back to the place we'd first entered.

That's what we did all day: pick up stones, push the cart, dump the stones, push the cart. Around and around. Hour after hour. No rest except the relief of pushing the empty cart. My back and shoulders ached. My hands stung from the cuts.

No food or water. I had a piece of bread saved from the day before. From time to time, I licked off a little bit and held it in my mouth. I never swallowed it right away. It felt better to have something in my mouth.

Early in the morning on the third day, big four-engine planes flew over and dropped bombs. The *Kapos* must have had some warning, because they yelled at us to stay inside the tunnels. Heavy explosions went on for several minutes. When they ended, we went outside.

The rails were twisted in places, compressors and other equipment turned over, pieces scattered over the ground. Some trees had burned.

The raid didn't damage anything inside the mountain, but it gave me hope. It was a sign the Germans were losing. And also it gave me some rest, because we couldn't work until the outside damage was repaired.

For the next nine days, I stayed in camp at Dora, doing nothing. I didn't know the day or even the month. Nobody had a calendar, and the days were all alike.

I asked Jacob, "What month do you think it is?"

"I don't know. It's been cold a long time. It's probably late in January, or maybe February. I'm sure it's 1945."

"Yes, I'm sure it is. I can count the winters."

Nobody was sure, but most of us thought it was February 1945.

One morning, even earlier than usual, the *Kapos* yelled at us to get up for roll call. We endured the same screaming and hitting. By now, it seemed almost normal. It was like the morning we left Jawiszowice, thousands of prisoners standing in rows of five, waiting to hear our numbers, waiting to get into trucks parked on the road outside the gate.

After daybreak, the trucks drove into the camp. As soon as one was loaded with people, it left.

Ice was frozen on the edges of the truck bed, and I was afraid I'd slip and bang my knee again.

A young man waited to climb up.

"Please," I said to him. "I've got a bad knee. If I hit it again, I won't be able to walk. Please help me get in."

"Sure," he said. "Put your foot on my hands, and I'll push."

His name was Moishe. We stood next to each other in the crowded truck and started talking about our families. That's what everybody talked about.

"I had two brothers," he said, "and a sister, all younger than me. The Germans grabbed me in the street one day. I never had a chance to tell them goodbye. God knows what happened to them! And my parents! Maybe they're dead. If they are, they're better off than we are."

"They might be," I said. "But if we can survive a little longer, maybe we'll make it."

The truck went along a bumpy, dirt road for about two hours before it stopped.

"Get out!" a guard shouted. "You walk the rest of the way."

"I hope it's not very far," I said to Moishe. "I know my knee won't hold up."

"I'll help you if you can't make it," he said.

We climbed down. It was only a few minutes until the guard stopped us, but on every step my knee felt like somebody had stuck it with a sharp knife.

"I don't know why the truck didn't come all the way," I said. "The road's no rougher here than what we rode on."

"No reason, probably. They're bastards."

A high gate was in front of us, with a sign that read *Krawinkel*[1] *Lager*. The gate swung open, and we walked in.

CHAPTER TWENTY ONE

Krawinkel *Dogs*

I'd never seen so many dogs. Every guard, every *Kapo* held a leash with a German shepherd lunging at us. More dogs were tied to gate posts. They growled and snarled as we went past, but they couldn't reach us.

"Please, God," I prayed, "don't let them get loose. I've come so far. Don't let dogs kill me now."

We stopped between rows of barracks, small ones different from any I'd seen before. They looked more like houses. An SS man called numbers and assigned groups of thirty to each barrack.

When we went in, I was disappointed that the bunks were only two rows high. The top row was close to the ceiling, but still too easy for a *Kapo* or guard to reach. I climbed up and lay curled into a ball. It was bitterly cold, and I shivered under the single blanket.

In the morning, we had bread and hot coffee. Not real coffee, more like mud-water, but the heat felt good on my hands and in my stomach.

A man next to me in the line asked my name.

"David Faber," I said.

"Faber? Maybe you have family here. The camp doctor is Faber also."

"Do you know his given name?"

"Hmmm," he hesitated. "I think it's Avram."

"He might be," I said.

It would be wonderful to find a relative, someone who knew my parents, someone who remembered.

The *Kapo*'s voice broke in.

"You'll all be assigned to the same job. Tomorrow morning."

Maybe I could see Dr. Faber, I thought, and find out if he really was a relative.

"How can I find the doctor?" I asked the man who told me about him.

"He's usually in the building across the street," he said.

"I'm going to look for him. Thanks for telling me."

I walked across the cement street and went into another little barrack. A man, forty or so, looked up from where he sat at a small, wooden desk.

"What do you want?" He didn't sound friendly.

"Are you Dr. Faber?" I asked.

"Yes. What do you want?"

"My name is David Faber, and maybe we're related. Where are you from?"

"From Nowy Sącz."

"Oh, I was born there! Did you know my mother, Eva Faber?"

"Yes. She was my father's sister."

"Then we're cousins!" I smiled at him.

He didn't smile back. His voice was cold as he asked, "Is that what you wanted to know?"

"Yes."

"All right. Now please go."

He looked down at some papers on the desk. I hated him! How could he treat family like that? I turned and walked out.

The next morning, the *Kapo* handed out a shovel to everyone else in my barrack, and they went off to work somewhere. I didn't know why I was left behind. Maybe my cousin was doing something for me after all. Maybe he just had to be careful. Then I got scared. Maybe they were going to kill me because I had a bad knee and couldn't work hard. That probably was it.

The *Kapo* called to me.

"*Komm her, du Kleiner.* You stay, you have a different job."

We went back into the barrack and waited. After a few minutes, an SS man carrying a rifle and holding a dog on a leash opened the door and stepped inside. The *Kapo* jumped to his feet and stood at attention.

"Which *Schweinehund* do you have for me?"

"This little one, sir."

The German looked at me.

"*Du kommst mit mir.*"

"*Jawohl, mein Herr!*"

"I will show you what you have to do. Did you understand me?"

"*Jawohl, mein Herr!* I understand."

My knee made it hard for me to keep up with him as we walked toward a huge building, like the ones at Auschwitz. He held the dog on the other side of him, but it kept lunging toward me and snarling.

I began to hear other dogs barking, faintly at first and then louder and louder as we got near the barrack. It must be full of dogs, I thought. What is he going to do with me? I'm scared of these dogs, afraid to be near them. I wished they'd given me a shovel.

He opened the single door in the middle of the long wall. The noise of barking and growling hit me like a hard blow. We went inside, and I saw dogs chained to all the walls.

"This is your job," the SS man said.

I shivered, terrified.

"You'll feed these dogs. Take good care of them or I'll take care of you. Understand?"

"*Jawohl, mein Herr!*"

"*Komm!*"

We went outside, and he closed the door. My ears rang from the barking, but at least I was away from the dogs. We walked to the left a short distance to a small barrack like the one I slept in.

It smelled good when we went inside, and it was warm. It was a kitchen, with huge kettles on top of the stoves. Small pots filled with food sat by each of the kettles. There was a wonderful smell, one that I hadn't known for years.

Big slabs of meat hung from hooks. Some of it looked like beef. I thought some of it might be horsemeat. Bags of potatoes lay in piles on the floor, along with white sugar beets and other vegetables.

The guard said, "Somebody will help you load the soup on this truck. You take it to the dogs."

"*Jawohl, mein Herr!*"

He helped me put two kettles on the wooden hand truck.

"Take this now and feed them. There are bowls on a shelf by the door. Fill a bowl for each dog. You understand?"

"*Jawohl, mein Herr!*"

He held open the door, and I pushed the cart outside. It was heavy and my knee wobbled, but I kept going back toward the dogs. The SS man said nothing as he turned and went in the other direction.

The noise of the dogs poured over me when I opened the barrack door and peered in. Oh, my God, I thought, how can I ever feed these dogs? They'll rip me apart. There were at least a hundred dogs, separated by wire nets fastened to long boards so they couldn't fight one another. It reminded me of a stable I'd seen once.

I decided to taste the food before I filled the bowls. It was delicious. I could taste the sugar beets, beans, and chunks of meat. I didn't know what kind of meat, and I didn't care. I took some more. At least, I told myself, I won't be hungry when they rip me apart! The feel of the food in my mouth and going down into my stomach was so good it made me cry.

The dogs kept barking, and I got more and more scared of them. But I had to feed them. The SS man probably would give me to them if I didn't. I saw a broom by the door. That gave me an idea. I pushed the cart down the right-hand side of the building all the way to the other end, filled a bowl, set it on the floor, and with the broom pushed it close to the dog. That way he couldn't reach me.

I kept going from one side to the other, filling the bowls and pushing them with the broom. With every bowlful, I put a bite in my mouth, too.

It got quiet as the dogs ate. There was no barking, just the rattle of bowls on the floor and the sound of their chewing. The quiet and the food I ate made me less afraid.

I fed the dogs three times a day.

Stacks of boxes were just inside the door. One had the top torn off, and I could see beige-colored biscuits with holes in them. German words were on each one: *Hundebiskuits*—dog biscuits.

I was too full to eat any. I tied the bottom of both pants legs with a piece of string and dropped in a few biscuits. That night I shared them with Moishe and some of the men who slept near me.

The biscuits were too hard to chew, but we held them in our mouths until they slowly melted. They tasted good, and it took a long time to finish one. That way we could have something in our mouths for hours.

Everyone kept the secret for the three weeks I had that job.

Then came the same old story, an early-morning roll call. "Some of you are leaving this camp," the SS officer told us.

I hated to leave the good job with the dogs. I wasn't afraid of them anymore. And especially I hated losing their food. The soup and meat put weight back on me, and I'd become stronger. My knee didn't hurt much, and I felt good.

My cousin stood beside the camp commander. As each prisoner paused in front of him, the doctor decided whether or not the man could work. If he said "yes," the man stayed in camp. "No" meant he'd be sent somewhere else, probably to be gassed or shot.

My turn came, and I looked at my cousin.

"Please," I said, "please, I can work. I have a good job. Let me stay here."

He looked down and wrote my number on the list of those to be sent away.

CHAPTER TWENTY TWO

BERGEN-BELSEN AND LIBERATION

From Krawinkel, we were sent a few miles away to a concentration camp called Ohrdruf,[1] where we stayed for about two weeks. Then, like many times before, we had to get on a train.

This time we didn't wait on the station platform. As soon as the first people were off the train, guards yelled to start walking. Before long we came to a huge gate with high towers on each side and along the fences as far as I could see. Guards moved in the shadows behind the floodlights.

Belsen Concentration Camp,[2] another piece of hell. The war is almost over, I thought. If there is a God, please let me survive.

The gates opened, and we went in for a few hundred yards, walking between barbed-wire fences. Stacks of clothing and piles of shoes lay on both sides of the road. And bodies—hundreds and hundreds of naked bodies. They looked like piles of bones. I thought all of them were dead until I saw an arm rise and drop. I shuddered.

We waited before a second gate until guards opened it, yelling and beating anyone within reach. They stopped once we passed through and stood by a row of windowless barracks.

I shuffled to the open door of the closest building and looked inside. The smell of urine and feces gagged me, along with the smell that had filled the apartment in Tarnów, the smell of dead bodies.

There were no bunks. Bodies with arms and legs at odd angles or curled into tight balls almost covered the bare, wooden floor. Others leaned against the walls. Some were covered with what looked like a kind of sheet. I stepped inside and looked more closely. Lice.

Most of the men sitting against the walls seemed alive. Or half-alive. One lifted his head and stared at me with enormous eyes. His mouth hung open, and spit drooled across his chin.

I heard footsteps and turned to see a man wearing a prison uniform looking at me.

"You're a new one," he said. "You want some soup? You can help me."

I stared at him. "What do you do?"

He let out his breath.

"There's only one job. Clear out the dead ones."

"That's the only work here?"

"It's that or starve," he said.

He pushed his foot against a body sprawled near the door.

"This one's ready to go. Give me a hand."

He pulled a rope belt from the pants on a dead body and handed it to me. "Tie this around his legs and pull him to the oven. The *Kapo* will give you a little soup."

I took the rope and leaned over the corpse. My fingers touched the lice that covered the bony legs, and bile rose in my throat.

"I can't," I said. "I can't touch him."

"No work, no soup," he said. "If you don't want to end up the same way, you'll do it."

The war was almost over. I had to live. I swallowed hard, slipped the rope around his legs, and tied it as tightly as I could.

The man moved to another body and fastened a short rope around its legs.

"All right," he said. "Let's go."

I followed close behind him as we dragged the bodies a few hundred feet. I kept my eyes looking down and tried not to see what was sliding along the ground in front of me, not to think about what I was doing.

This oven was different from the big ones at Auschwitz. What looked like hundreds of bodies lay on top of one another alongside it, waiting to be burned. Every few minutes, two prisoners grabbed head and feet and shoved a body into the furnace.

"Here's a new one, sir," the man who had told me how to get food said to the *Kapo*. "Can he have a little soup?"

The man laughed. "I guess so. But he'll have to work a little more first."

We went to another barrack, this one with women and girl prisoners. My new friend pointed to a small body, naked, with almost no breasts, bones sticking up at ugly angles. Dirty-blonde hair was cut close to her skull. I wondered if she'd been pretty.

Again I tied the rope around the body and pulled it to the furnace. This time the *Kapo* spooned a little soup into a bowl and handed it to me.

"Here," he said. "You can have more when you've done more work."

The soup was thin and cold, but it eased the hurting in my stomach. Then the realization of how I'd gotten it and the smell of the burning flesh sickened me, and I vomited.

"You don't like the soup?" the *Kapo* sneered. "Well, maybe it will taste better in a few days."

I had to keep on. Maybe I'd die anyway, but this was my only chance. I went back to the barracks and dragged out more bodies. When the *Kapo* poured soup into my bowl at the end of the day, I managed to keep it down.

The next day it was harder and harder to pull the bodies, even though they weighed little. I became more and more feverish and by mid-afternoon had to stop. Now I'd be like the others. Before long, some new prisoner would drag me to the oven.

I saw Finci in Bergen-Belsen soon after I arrived. Then I didn't see him anymore. He must have died. He gave up on life after his father's murder.

One day, I slumped down outside the barrack. It felt like spring, with a warm sun on my face and body. I turned my head toward the man sitting next to me.

"I wonder what month it is," I said.

"I'm not sure, but it might be April. It's getting a little warmer."

April 1945, I thought. But what difference did it make? I wouldn't live more than a few weeks.

I stared across the concrete street. A small camp was there, on the other side of a barbed-wire fence. I'd seen people walking there, people who looked very different from us. They weren't Germans, at least no one wore an SS or Wehrmacht uniform. They wore nice clothes instead of prison rags. Men, women, and children were together, like families. And I noticed most of all that they didn't look hungry.

I must be out of my mind. The fever must be making me see

things that weren't there.

An elegantly dressed man with two children came close to the fence and threw pieces of bread onto the street. I scrambled to pick up some of it, but I was too weak to push through the crowd of men. Some people fell, and others stepped on them, fighting for the scraps of food. Like dogs, I thought.

The next day, the same thing happened. This time, I just watched.

The third morning, the little camp seemed deserted. I felt I must have been delirious, that I'd imagined it all. But that couldn't be. I'd felt people shoving me when I tried to get the bread. It had been real.

Other than the few scraps of bread that had been thrown over the fence the day before, there was no food anywhere in the camp. People became desperate. Some of those who were still alive started to eat the flesh of the dead. There were some horse wagons, and people pulled the metal parts off the wheels. They sharpened the metal on stones that they found, and then used the metal to cut away pieces of flesh to eat. There wasn't much flesh there, mainly just skin and bones. I felt my stomach turn, and I couldn't watch anymore.

I went back into the barrack and sat against a wall. A man who I thought was in his thirties lay to my right. His cheeks were hollow, but his belly looked fat.

"What's wrong with you?" I asked.

"Typhus."[3]

He used some medical words I didn't understand.

"I'm swelling because my body is full of water," he went on. "I won't last much longer."

"Can I do anything for you?"

"Nothing, boy. I'm a doctor, but I've got nothing to help you or myself. Just try to survive. You should go ahead and eat some of the flesh from the dead bodies, so you don't die."

"Then I'll die," I told him. "I just can't bring myself to do it."

"You must eat anything you can. If you can't eat flesh, then try eating grass. You'll also get some moisture from it, especially if you eat it in the morning," he said. "You're bleeding from the rectum. Looks like you're sick, too."

"Maybe I am."

"Take a little bit of soft wood," he said, pointing to a pile of broken lumber on the floor. He took a few matches from his pocket. "Burn the wood and eat the ashes. I have no medicine for you, but that will stop the bleeding."

"Thank you," I said, taking the matches and wondering how he had managed to get them.

Another man lay near my feet, eyes open, staring at nothing.

"Who are you?" I asked him. "Where are you from?"

"I come from Tarnów."

"Tarnów! That's where I'm from."

I pulled up the sleeve of his prison jacket and looked at the number tattooed on his arm. 161041—almost the same as mine.

"We must have been in the same transport," he said. "Where have you been? There are so many camps. But we're all going to die here."

Suddenly I felt determined to live.

"No!" I almost shouted. "I'm not giving up. The war is almost over. Please don't give up."

That night the doctor died, along with a lot of others, including most of those who had been eating the flesh from the dead bodies. I didn't want to stay in the barrack any longer. I wanted to get outside, into the sunshine and warm air. But I was too weak to stand, and my body burned with fever. I had to get water.

I pushed myself onto my hands and knees and slowly crawled outside to the water spigot, pushing my bowl in front of me. The Germans had turned off the water, but the valve was loose, and it still came through, a drop at a time. I set my bowl under the spigot until about a teaspoon of water covered the bottom, enough to wet my mouth. I crawled to a grassy area. It had rained recently, and the grass was very green and dewy. I was hungry, and I was dying. I ate the grass, like an animal.

I took the doctor's advice, burned a small piece of wood, and managed to swallow a bit of ash. I later noticed that I was not bleeding as much.

I lay there, watching men who still had some strength pull the dead out of the barracks. They didn't take them to the oven, just left them on the street.

Later that afternoon, I slid my back up the barrack wall until I was standing up. My knees buckled, and I slumped down again. I pushed myself up and this time took a few steps before falling to the ground. Finally, I quit trying to stand and crawled back inside.

The man from Tarnów was still alive, and I collapsed next to him.

"Where did you live in Tarnów?" I asked.

He gave me his address. It was close to my own home, and his parents had known mine.

"I remember all of you," he said. "Even you." He pulled back his lips in a smile that showed that almost all his teeth were gone. "You were the youngest. Isn't your name Faber?"

"Yes, David Faber. You have a good memory."

"I'm Chaim. I remember your family. What happened to them?"

I didn't think I could cry anymore, but tears came as I answered him.

"All gone. I may have a sister in England, but everyone else is dead. What about your family?"

He closed his eyes. "They're all gone, too," he said. "There's nothing to live for."

Suddenly we heard planes, like thunder. One after another, they kept coming. I crawled to the door and looked up. They didn't look like German planes. A fighter plane flew low over the camp, and I saw the round markings of the British air force.

Soon we heard gunfire, first every few minutes, then almost without a break. The heavy booming reminded me of the first night in Sosnowiec. It got louder and louder, and we could see the glare of fires against the sky.

By morning, the guns were very close. I crawled to the door and looked around. Something seemed different, but I didn't know what. I looked up at the guard towers. They were empty. The Germans were gone.

I looked over a fence to an empty camp. A white pigeon was sitting on the wire that was strung between the fence's wooden spikes. The pigeon looked just like my Kubush back in Tarnów. It turned its head back and forth and seemed to be cooing to me. I was feverish and sick. I looked again to the empty camp on the other side of the fence, but my gaze was brought back to the bird, which was now sitting on top of some dead bodies. The pigeon stayed there for a few minutes, cooed again, then flew away. I never saw it again.

I closed my eyes and waited.

I told myself that we'd soon be free, but for hours nothing happened. Then I heard trucks roaring into camp. Soon after, tanks creaked and rumbled behind them.

A prisoner burst through the door.

"We're free!" he shouted. "The Americans are here!"

It was what I'd told myself would happen soon, but I couldn't let myself believe it.

"Please," I said, "don't make a joke. Let us die in peace. Please get out of here."

He ran out still shouting, "We're free! We're free!"

A few minutes later, another man came inside and shouted, "The British are here!"

This time, I had to believe it. Two people wouldn't make the same awful joke. And the guards were gone.

Sobs shook my body. "I did it, Mama!" I stammered. "I survived!"

Get out, I thought. I have to get out of here. They'll think I'm dead if I stay inside. I couldn't walk, but I pushed myself up onto my hands and knees. It was only about ten feet to the door; I could get there. Slowly I shoved one hand ahead a few inches, then pulled myself forward. Again. My body shook and I collapsed, my cheek pressed against the dirty floor.

I lay quietly a few minutes before trying again. It was no use. I couldn't do it. I'd die there with the others.

Heavy footsteps sounded near me, and I looked up at a soldier standing just inside the door. He stared at the filthy bodies for a moment, then shouted in German, "Men! You're free!"

My throat was so dry I could scarcely talk, but I had to make him hear me. With the little strength I had, I forced out, "Help!" I wasn't much more than a loud whisper, and he seemed not to hear me. I tried again, and this time he turned and looked at me.

He stepped closer, knelt at my side, and laid his rifle on the floor. "Hang on, boy," he said. "Just hang on. You're going to be all right. I'm going for help. I'll be right back."

He picked up his rifle and went out. A few minutes later, two other soldiers came in. This time, their message was in different languages: German, Polish, French. "You're free!"

"You're going to a hospital. We'll take care of you." Beautiful words!

I knew what they were saying, but it was hard to believe that we really were getting out of hell. Maybe I was just seeing things and hearing voices because of my fever. I wanted to believe, but still I was afraid I'd wake up and find everything the same.

I heard loudspeakers blaring the same words, again in several languages. It was too much to be a delusion. It had to be true.

"Chaim," I said, "come on. We have to get out of here, away from all these dead people. They'll pick us up sooner if we're outside and take us to a hospital."

Chaim groaned. He said something in a low voice I couldn't understand. I leaned over him. "Chaim, we'll die if we stay here. We have to get outside."

"I can't move," he whispered. "Save yourself. Too late."

I touched his face. "All right," I told him. "I'll tell them to come get you."

He closed his eyes and smiled. I hated to leave him, but I couldn't move him. "I'll tell them, Chaim," I said again.

A few feet at a time, I crawled around the dead and the dying. It seemed hours before I made it outside and lay by the edge of the asphalt road.

Tanks clanked by a few feet from my head. A man near me crawled onto the road and lay there. A tank stopped, and a soldier climbed down and moved him to one side. The man grabbed the soldier's hand and kissed it. The soldier touched the man's head, got back onto the tank, and rode away.

Brakes squeaked, and an open army car stopped close to me. Two women got out, dressed in blue skirts and jackets.

One of them, tall, thin, with a long face, knelt and spoke to me in German. I saw the Red Cross band on her arm.

"You'll be all right, boy. We'll help you. Do you understand me?"

"*Ja,*" I said.

She held her palm against my forehead, frowned, and said something in English to the shorter woman standing next to her.

Again she spoke to me in German. "I'm Mrs. Crosthwaite from the British Red Cross. This is Mrs. Montgomery.[4] We'll take you to the hospital."

She put her arms under my shoulders, and Mrs. Montgomery helped lift me into the back of the car. The shorter woman leaned over me, her face framed by grey bangs and long, straight hair. She smiled and touched my face.

"Let's go." Mrs. Crosthwaite was already seated behind the steering wheel. Mrs. Montgomery got in beside her, and we drove away. The motion of the car nauseated me, and I passed out.

Dimly, I heard a woman speaking German, and I felt a wet cloth sliding over my body. Eyes closed, I tried to figure out where I was. The last thing I remembered was riding in the open car and feeling sick. Now I lay on a hard surface while someone washed me.

The muttering voice became clearer.

"Look at this filthy little Jew! What pigs they are!"

Suddenly rage enveloped me. I opened my eyes and saw a broad-faced peasant woman bending over me. Without thinking, I grabbed her hair with both hands and knocked her head against the hard surface I lay on. Twice, three times. All the while, she screamed and jerked against my grip.

Exhausted, I let loose and let my arms drop to my sides.

Red-faced, the German turned to the Red Cross woman who stood nearby.

"You saw what he did!" she shouted. "The animal!"

"I don't blame him," the other woman said. "See that you get him clean."

The peasant woman made a face but said no more as she washed my legs and feet. I slipped back into unconsciousness before she finished.

CHAPTER TWENTY THREE

REHABILITATION

I woke and heard someone, a man, singing in English. I lay quietly for a moment, listening, telling myself that it wasn't a dream. I opened my eyes and saw a young soldier standing at the foot of my bed. It was a real bed, with clean sheets and a pillow! I rolled my head from one side to the other and saw more beds, some empty, some with men lying in them.

The man stopped singing, smiled, and came to my side. He spoke words I didn't understand, turned, and left the room. In a few minutes he came back, holding a bowl in one hand, a spoon in the other.

Sitting on the bed, he fed me a few spoonfuls of hot soup. I tried to tell him I was hungry and wanted more, but he shook his head and walked away with the bowl.

I looked around at the other beds. This must be a hospital. That's where the Red Cross ladies said they were taking me. I was safe. The war was over. But I was very hungry. Why wouldn't the soldier give me more to eat?!

A British officer came a little later and in broken German told me that he was a doctor.

"Why can't I have more to eat?" I asked him. "I'm hungry, and all he'd give me was a little soup."

"Only a little at a time for a while," he said. "You had typhus, and if you eat a lot, you'll die."

He didn't understand. I had survived typhus; now I needed food to get back my strength. I had to do something to get food. When both the doctor and the soldier had gone from the room, I got to my feet, pulled a blanket from the bed, wrapped it around my naked body, and walked out into a hall.

A stairway was close by, and I went down it to the ground floor. Nobody saw me as I slipped out the door and looked around. Nearby was what looked like a stable. I hurried to an open door and went inside, where I found dirty clothes someone had left. I put them on and walked unnoticed past the guardhouse at the gate. Surely I could find something to eat.

All kinds of war wreckage lay along the road: burned-out trucks and tanks, bits of uniforms, and guns. I picked up a German machine gun and held it under my arm. It was broken, but it looked dangerous, and I felt safer with it.

The gun was heavy, and I began to tremble. I had to find food quickly or I'd collapse. A house was just down the road a little way. Maybe I could make it that far. I half-walked, half-stumbled along until I reached the house and, without knocking, jerked open the door.

A man, a woman, and a young girl sat at a wooden table. The girl screamed, and the man started to stand.

"Stay where you are!" I shouted in German. Pointing the gun at the woman, I went on. "Get me food, quick, or I'll kill all of you."

The woman hesitated, then picked up the loaf of bread from the table and held it out to me.

"I want more than that. You Germans starved me. Now you'll give me food."

The woman went to a cupboard and took out jam, butter, and a piece of meat. "Put it in a sack and lay it on the table," I told her. "Then all of you stand on the other side of the room. Hurry!" I didn't know how long I could stand there holding the machine gun.

She put the sack on the table, and I noticed the gold wedding ring on her finger. "Put that ring in the sack, too," I said. Maybe I could trade it for more food later on. The Germans took Mama's gold wedding chain. I was just getting back a little part of it.

Slowly I reached out, picked up the sack, and held it in one hand while I backed to the door. All the time the gun was pointed at them. No one followed as I went to the road and headed back toward the hospital. On the way I stopped, broke off a piece of bread, and stuffed it into my mouth. It was fresh and warm, delicious.

Again, no one at the guardhouse paid any attention to me as I walked past, trying not to show how nervous I was.

For a few days, I feasted on the stolen food and felt my strength increase. Then the hunger returned, and I had to look for food again.

By this time, I'd learned that there was a central kitchen where food was cooked for the whole hospital. That would be a good place to start looking. I went to the back door, wanting to go in but afraid to do it. An officer saw me standing there, came outside, and spoke in English.

"Hunger," I answered. "Hunger." Please, make him understand.

"Hungry?"

"Yes! Yes! Hungry!"

He motioned for me to follow him inside and down into the basement. There, he pointed to a pile of coal and then to two buckets. I understood he wanted me to fill the buckets and take them upstairs to the kitchen stoves.

Still weak, I was exhausted by the time I filled the buckets and dragged one of them to the bottom of the steep stairway. I tried to go up with it, but I couldn't.

The officer looked at me, then picked up both buckets and carried them up the stairs. He set them down and led me to a table.

"Sit," he said, pointing to a chair.

He brought a big dish of rice, bread and butter, and coffee. Like an animal, I stuffed the food into my mouth as fast as I could. Suddenly the back of my pants felt wet, and I knew I was bleeding. I said nothing, just kept on eating.

Every day after that, I went to the kitchen, and the captain gave me food. By the end of a week, I was much stronger, and I'd learned enough English to communicate a little.

"I can work now," I told him, "work for food."

The captain told me to wash potatoes. I did that for a few days and then worked at a lot of different jobs. Finally he let me cook, and soon I was preparing most of the food for the officers' mess.

Mrs. Crosthwaite and Mrs. Montgomery came to see me. I told them about my sister Rachel going to England before the war, and they promised to try to find her.

About a month later, one of the men who lived in Block 16 with me ran up, yelling.

"David! David! There's someone here to see you! Some family!"

Family! I couldn't believe it. I ran to the door and saw a

man wearing the uniform of a British officer. He smiled and spoke in Polish.

"David, my name is Leo Wachtel. I am your sister's husband, Rachel's husband."

My sister's husband! I threw my arms around him, and he hugged me in return. Then we sat on a low wall close by and talked for an hour or more. He told me that he was one of the Polish soldiers in Anders' Army.[1] He'd escaped from Cracow into Russia, then gone to England, where he met Rachel.

He took a snapshot of another woman from his pocket, and showed it to me. "Have you ever seen this young lady?" he asked.

I looked at the photograph. My God! I almost fainted. "Excuse me a minute," I stammered. "I need a drink of water."

I went to the bathroom for water. Suddenly my knees buckled, and I fell. After lying on the floor a few minutes, I got up, washed my face in cold water, and went back outside.

"Are you all right?" Leo looked worried.

"Yes, I'm all right. I just needed a drink."

He held out the picture.

"Yes, Leo," I said. "I know who that is. Who is that girl to you?"

"She's my sister," he said.

I put my hand on his arm. "I'm very sorry, Leon, but she's gone. She was taken away in a transport. Please don't ask me how it happened. It's over, and I don't want to have to remember."

"How did you know her?"

"You remember your sister was going to be married to a man in Tarnów?"

"Yes, I remember. That's why she went there."

"She was going to marry my cousin, my mother's brother's son. My family was in Tarnów at Uncle Hanoh's place when the Germans picked up your sister."

Leo sat quietly for a few minutes. "Thank you for telling me," he finally said. "It's better to know what happened."

I hated lying to him. She didn't go with a transport. She was killed saving my life when the Germans broke into Uncle Hanoh's apartment. That's why I broke down when I saw Helen's picture. I was afraid to tell Leo the truth, afraid he would hate me and not help me get to England.

Leo had lost his sister while I had regained mine.

David Faber's family photo

This photo of David Faber [c. 1946] was taken about a year after liberation from Bergen-Belsen.

EPILOGUE

After the War

After the liberation from Belsen, I went to Kalé in France, then in 1946 from France to Dover, England. On the ship to Dover, I seemed to be the only civilian. I took a train to London, and eventually found my sister.

I was finally reunited with Rachel. She and her husband gave me a heartfelt welcome, but I found it impossible to adjust to living with people who had not experienced the horrors of Nazi concentration camps. After a few weeks, I left my sister's home to find quarters in a bomb-damaged building. I discovered that I also had trouble adjusting to life, in general. I had survived so many concentration camps, but after the war I was sometimes very nervous.

Shortly after settling in London, I saw a policeman. At first I thought he was a German, and my instincts took over. I started to run away, but the policeman ran after me. When the officer caught up with me, he took me to the police station, and I spent at least half the day in jail. I was taken to a judge, who asked me why I had run away. I told the judge about having survived the death camps, showed him the tattooed numbers on my arm, and explained that I had been afraid that the policeman was a German. By the time I finished telling the judge my story, he had tears in his eyes. He gave me a hug and said, "You are now in a free country." The policeman I had earlier been afraid of was also crying, and invited me to his house to meet his family. He then became my friend. Every week, he came to see me, bringing me chocolate and fruit. He was about 40 years old, much older than I was. He was my first friend in London.

I also met the man I had seen throwing bread over the fence at Bergen-Belsen. When I stayed with my sister, the street we lived on was Black Lion Yard, which was really just a narrow alley. I recognized this man with his the two children, and I walked over to him.

"Excuse me, sir," I said, "my English is not so good. May I ask you a question, please?"

"Go ahead," he said.

"Are you by any chance the man who threw the bread over the fence at Bergen-Belsen?" I asked. "Maybe I was imagining things, or maybe I was feverish."

"Yes, I was. We were used," he said, "as exchange for high-ranking German officers."

It turned out that this man was British. He had been visiting family in Poland and got stuck there. The Nazis had isolated him and his children, but in better conditions than the part of the camp I was in. The Nazis kept them well fed, so that Germany could exchange them for high-ranking German officer POWs. There were many such families there.

When the Allies were closing in on Bergen-Belsen toward the end of the war, the Germans had apparently realized they were losing the war and locked up many of the American and British families inside of train boxcars before abandoning the camp.

THE FATE OF WAR CRIMINALS

Romek's killer, the Gestapo officer Otto Grunow, has been missing since 1945, and is presumed dead.[1] His accomplice, Wilhelm Rommelmann, was sentenced to death by a Polish court in Tarnów in 1948.[2]

Information relating to Romek's activities in the Polish Underground are apparently still classified, and recent attempts at getting more information from the American, German, and Polish governments have been unsuccessful. Extensive research into this matter has shown that Romek was, in fact, a member of the Polish Army and in 1939 had been a prisoner of war at Buchenwald – the same camp where David Faber was later held captive.

Since the war, new information from the British National Archives and other sources regarding shipments of heavy water into Germany have also surfaced, including Polish Underground sabotaging of German transports.

Over the years, David has been a witness in the investigations and trials of many Nazi war criminals.

MRS. CROSTHWAITE [left; photo c. 1946] and MRS. MONTGOMERY, the British Red Cross volunteers who rescued David Faber during the April 15, 1945, liberation of Bergen-Belsen Concentration Camp and later helped him find his sister Rachel in London (Chapters 22 and 23).

MRS. CROSTHWAITE [standing center, in hat; photo c. 1946]; MRS. MONTGOMERY [seated]; and CAPTAIN BLAKE [left seated], the British captain in charge of the kitchen at Bergen-Belsen where David Faber worked during his rehabilitation (Chapter 23).

The two photographs of Mrs. Crosthwaite and Mrs. Montgomery on the preceding page are from the collection of Mrs. Montgomery, who bequeathed them to her niece Margaret (Mrs. John Collinson). Mr. and Mrs. Collinson gave them to David Faber in March 2000 when he visited Scotland at the invitation of Lady Melanie Landale, President of the British Red Cross, Dumfries and Galloway Branch, to address the Annual Branch Assembly.

Sir David Landale KCVO, husband of Lady Landale, is a nephew of Mrs. Crosthwaite. He provided the photograph of Mrs. Crosthwaite on the following page and shared with David Faber details about her later life, including that she "latterly became Mrs. Ian Ker, her first husband having been killed in the war" (personal communication, June 16, 1998).

MRS. CROSTHWAITE [Mrs. Ian Ker], many years after World War II, outside Buckingham Palace on the day she was awarded the Member of the British Empire from HM Queen Elizabeth, accompanied by her nephews, Sir David Landale [left] and Major David McMicking.

Mrs. Crosthwaite is wearing a British Red Cross uniform with medals, including one for her work at Belsen.

A New Life

Paul Grachstein, the Jawiszowice camp electrician, survived the war and moved to Israel, where David met him many years later. Paul turned out to be a cousin of David's first wife, Tonia.

David went to England late in 1946 and was reunited with his sister. A few months later, Tonia, a Jewish girl from Poland whom David had met in Bergen-Belsen, came to London to live with an uncle. Shaped by common suffering, David and Tonia were drawn to one another. They married and lived in England for eleven years. David learned to be a pastry chef and worked in a number of places, including the kitchen of the House of Commons, serving the likes of former Prime Minister Winston Churchill.

With their only son, David and Tonia immigrated to the United States in 1957. They lived for a short time in New York City and for twenty years in Springfield, Massachusetts, finally moving to San Diego, California in 1978.

Tonia died suddenly on Thanksgiving night 1986, and David was alone again after forty years of a happy marriage.

David is now married to Lina, who is also a Holocaust victim. They live in San Diego, near her children and grandchildren, so that he is once again a member of a large and loving family.

REFERENCES AND NOTES

PROLOGUE

[1] **Katowice**
South-central Polish city, part of the Silesia province, which belonged to Prussia prior to WWI. The city became part of Poland in 1922, though much of the population there still spoke German, which was the predominant language of Prussia. David was born in the city of Nowy Sącz, Poland. He and his family moved to Katowice when David was seven years old.

[2] **Panzer divisions**
Military divisions of armored tanks used by the Germans during WWII.

[3] **Ulica**
"Street" in the Polish language.

[4] **Synagogue**
Jewish house of worship.

CHAPTER 1

[1] **Wilhelm von Keudell**, of the German consulate, contacted David Faber on several occasions, regarding the investigations and prosecutions of various Nazi war criminals, as evidenced by letters from von Keudell which David saved.

[2] *Yiddish*
Language spoken by Jews of central and eastern European origin. Prior to WWII, most European Jews spoke Yiddish at home, though outside of the home they may also have spoken the predominant language (i.e., German, Polish) of their respective countries.

[3] **Senator Jacob Javits (1904-1986)**
Republican senator representing New York State, who was also Jewish.

[4] **Shipments of heavy water**
Heavy water is an isotopic form of water, also known as deuterium oxide, which is used as a moderator in some nuclear reactors. The significance of heavy water to the building of the atomic bomb is described in many physics textbooks and encyclopedias, such as Musset and Lloret's *Concise Encyclopedia of the Atom*. Attempts of the Allies to sabotage German efforts to make the atomic bomb are less well known, but some reports have become declassified in recent years. For example, the British National Archives recently declassified

information about Polish Underground involvement in sabotaging German transports of various supplies and weapons, including a photo showing Polish soldiers standing in front of a derailed German train (National Archives of England, Wales and the United Kingdom, Document Reference HS 8/437). In addition, some Allied efforts of sabotaging heavy-water production by the Germans is well-documented, such as the Allied destruction of the heavy-water plant Norsk Hydro in German-occupied Norway in 1943.

[5] *Hauptsturmführer*
A German military ranking.

[6] **Wehrmacht**
The German armed forces of the years prior to and during World War II. The Wehrmacht, which was not affiliated with the SS or Gestapo, was until recently viewed as an army of individuals not associated with war crimes.

[7] **Gestapo**
The police force of Nazi Germany. The Gestapo's primary role was to get rid of any opposition to the Nazis within Germany and its occupied territories. The Gestapo was also responsible for capturing Jews and other "undesirables," and sending them to concentration camps.

CHAPTER 2

[1] **a POW camp called Buchenwald**
In July 2004, the Central Tracing Agency of the International Committee of the Red Cross in Geneva, Switzerland, forwarded a record of Abraham Faber having been a prisoner of war. According to a German report dated November 11, 1939, he was present in Stalag III-A (a subcamp of Buchenwald), and had the prisoner number 1757. The record also shows that he was born in Nowy Sącz on September 30, 1916.

Buchenwald is well known as a concentration camp but not so well known as a prisoner of war camp. Faber describes Romek's short imprisonment in Buchenwald in 1939. Romek was not only a Jew but also a Polish soldier. It was in his capacity as a Polish soldier and prisoner of war that Romek was released from Buchenwald.

> Buchenwald ... with 130 satellite camps ... [was] established July 16, 1937.... [The] "tent camp" [was] set up for Polish prisoners sent there after the German invasion of Poland in 1939.... The outbreak of war was accompanied by a wave of arrests ... followed by the influx of thousands of Poles.... (Gutman, *Encyclopedia of the Holocaust*, vol. 1, p. 254)

> Buchenwald ... In the wake of the Anschluss in March 1938, prisoners ... from all the occupied countries followed, although the great majority

were from Poland ... primarily political and Jewish prisoners. However, the raids against actual or presumed resistance fithters (especially in Poland) were so sweeping that all segments of the population were affected, regardless of political conviction or involvement with concrete political actions.... (Gutman, vol. 1, p. 311)

Buchenwald was one of the first concentration camps in Germany, and its inmates consisted initially of political prisoners and other targeted groups, including Jews. However, some of the prisoners were released, on the condition that they leave Germany. ("Buchenwald." Encyclopædia Britannica. 2004. Encyclopædia Britannica Online. 29 March 2004 <http://search.eb.com/eb/article?eu=18126>.

[2] **Talmud**
The ancient, sacred writings of Orthodox Judaism, which represents religious authority.

[3] **tallis**
A shawl traditionally worn by Jewish males, especially during prayer.

[4] **Bar Mitzvah**
The ceremony that initiates a 13-year-old Jewish boy into adulthood, thereby recognized in Jewish tradition as an adult who is responsible for his moral and religious duties.

[5] *Ja*
"yes" in the German language.

[6] **Führer**
Adolf Hitler took this title, which means "the leader" in the German language.

[7] *Schwein*
"Pig" in the German language.

[8] **the menorah, and the Kiddush cup in the Shabbat...**
A menorah is a candelabrum that holds seven or nine candles, and is used in Jewish worship. A Kiddush cup is a ceremonial cup or goblet, traditionally used during blessing and prayer over food or wine for the Sabbath , festivals, or religious holidays. Shabbat is the Jewish Sabbath, observed from sundown on Friday until sundown on Saturday.

CHAPTER 3

[1] **Hasidic coats, curls swinging**
A Hasid is a member of an ultra-orthodox sect of Judaism. Hassidic men traditionally have beards, grow side curls in their hair, keep their heads covered

with a hat, and wear dark-colored, conservative clothing.

[2] **yarmulke**

Also known as a "kippah," a yarmulke skullcap worn by Jewish men and boys, usually those of Orthodox or Conservative sects of Judaism.

CHAPTER 5

[1] *Sh'ma Yisrael...*

From Deuteronomy 6:5-9 of the Torah (Hebrew scriptures). The *Sh'ma* is traditionally recited twice a day by religious Jews, but tradition also holds that it is spoken as the dying words of Jewish martyrs.

CHAPTER 7

[1] *groszy*

A *grosz* is a subunit of the Polish basic unit of money, *zloty*. One *zloty* equals 100 *groszy*.

[2] **By the rules of war, they couldn't kill me in a POW camp.**

In 1929, representatives of many nations – including Germany, France, Great Britain, and the United States – met in Geneva, Switzerland, and agreed to the Geneva Convention Relating to the Treatment of Prisoners of War. The convention required prisoners of war (POWs) to be treated humanely, to have information provided about them, and to permit official visits to POW camps by representatives of neutral states. ("Geneva Conventions." Encyclopædia Britannica. 2004. Encyclopædia Britannica Online. 30 June 2004 <http://search.eb.com/eb/article?eu=37105>.

CHAPTER 8

[1] **Pustkow** was officially established in 1943. Faber describes being a prisoner there in 1940, and another former inmate describes being there in 1939 (see below). That the camp was not "established" until 1943 does not conflict with, but in fact supports, Faber's description that when he was at Pustkow the camp was not yet built. By chopping down trees and making clearings, he was among the prisoners building the camp.

> **PUSTKOW:** pow. Debica ... Poland ... CC Heidelager established Aug./Sept. 1943 ... training camp "Heidelager" of the Wehrmacht (Weinmann, *Das nationalsozialistische Lagersystem (CCP)*, p. 592).

> DEBICA: ... Poland ... FLC: First jentioned in Nov. 39 with its subcamp **Pustkow** (former inmate) (Weinmann, p. 592)

The map coordinates place Pustkow within a day's drive from Tarnów, as Faber describes.

> **Pustkow:** Pol.... 101 km WNW of Przemysl; 50°09'/21°30'
> (Mokotoff and Sack, *Where Once We Walked*, p. 276).

[2] *Schweinehunde*

   Literally, "pig-dogs" in the German language.

[3] *Kapo*

   In Nazi concentration camps, a *kapo* was a prisoner, often a Jew, who was in charge of groups of inmates.

[4] ...**wondering if it was pork**

   In Judaism, dietary laws prohibit the consumption of any food that is not *kosher*, that is any food not conforming to the dietary laws. Pork is not kosher, and is therefore not eaten by religious Jews.

CHAPTER 9

[1] **partisans**

   Soviet/Russian underground resistance movement, known for sabotaging German military activities during WWII. The partisans were well known for their forest encampments, which they used for strategic advantage.

CHAPTER 10

[1] **boric-acid water**

   Boric acid is typically available in a white, powder form. It can be diluted in water, and the solution is commonly used as an antiseptic or eye wash. Boric acid is also common in many industrial chemicals, including cosmetics.

[2] **Star of David**

   A six-pointed star, symbolizing Judaism.

[3] **Torah**

   The five books of Moses, Jewish scripture.

CHAPTER 11

[1] **into a ghetto, just like the old days**

   Throughout the centuries, many European cities created ghettos into which Jews were forcibly relocated.

[2] **Matzos** are flat pieces of brittle, unleavened, flat bread, usually eaten during the Jewish holiday of Passover.

³ **Kittel**
 In Judiaism, a white robe usually worn by men during synagogue services, major holidays, and religious festivals.

CHAPTER 12

¹ **They were always in the ghetto whenever anything bad happened.**
 Many of the war crimes committed by **Grunow** and **Rommelmann** are well documented. For example, in an interview dated January 12, 1946, a female Holocaust survivor described atrocities committed by Grunow and Rommelmann at the Tarnów Ghetto. The following is an English translation of an excerpt from the interview, which was originally conducted in Polish, by staff at Sweden's Lund University Polish Documentary Institute:

> When we returned from work, we were checked at the gate to see (checks were also carried out at work) whether we had brought anything to eat from the Polish side. Two Gestapo, Grunow and Rommelmann, were particularly eager during these checks and immediately shot dead those on whom, for example, white flour or cigarettes were found. These two Gestapo were busy in the ghetto all the time, always on the lookout for victims in their homes. They took out those unfortunates to the assembly area (a square where roll calls were held to count the work columns) and executed them. Also, if they found people praying - they executed some of them.

> Printed with permission: Saml. Lakocinski,Z. PIZ. Testimony no.111. Lund University Library

CHAPTER 13

¹ **Avrumaleh**
 A Yiddish endearment of the name Avrum (also Avram), which is the Yiddish form of Abraham.
² *Kluskis* are a type of dumpling, common in Polish cuisine.

³ **Valerian** is a plant whose rootstalk is used as a tonic in folk and natural medicines.

CHAPTER 14

¹ **Babcia**
 "Grandmother" in the Polish language.

[2] *Reichsdeutscher*
A German of the old German Empire. The German Empire was commonly known as the *Reich* until WWII.

[3] **Szebnia** (Szebnie) was located in Poland and closed in the fall of 1943, with some of the prisoners being transferred to Auschwitz. This description supports Faber's account of going from Szebnia to Auschwitz.

> **SZEBNIE:** pow. Jaslo ... Poland ... Add: CC Szebnie, first mentioned 1943, closed Aug./ Sept. 1943, the skilled workers being transferred to CC "Heidelager"-Pustkow, and the others pris. To CC Auschwitz (Weinmann, p. 592).

> **Szebnie:** Pol....82 km WSW of Przemysl; 49°46'/21°36' (Mokotoff and Sack, p. 276).

[4] **Dybbuk**
In Jewish folklore, a demon or ghost that enters the body of a living person and controls his or her behavior.

CHAPTER 15

[1] **161051**
November 5, 1943: 4,237 Jewish men, women, and children from Szebnie labor camp arrive in an RSHA transport. After the selection, 952 men and 396 women are admitted to the camp and given Nos. 160879-161830 and 66702-67097. The remaining 2,889 people are killed in the gas chambers (Czech, *Auschwitz Chronicle 1939-1945*, p. 520).

David Faber's tattoo number 161051 is within the numeric series described above and fixes his Auschwitz arrival date at November 5, 1943. This date is consistent with Faber's description of arriving in cold weather. Moreover, the reference supports the series of details in Faber's description: arriving at Auschwitz by train from Szebnia (Szebnie), undergoing selection (the process of assigning prisoners to forced labor or immediate murder), receiving a tattoo number, and watching as, in Faber's words, "thousands were hauled away."

In the 1997 edition, the date of David Faber's arrival at Auschwitz was given as January 1943, an estimate based on the relative position of Auschwitz in the chain of concentration camps in which Faber was imprisoned, and on his estimate of the amount of time he spent in each, as well as on the fact that he arrived at Auschwitz in cold weather.

After the 1997 edition was published, Mr. Steven Vitto, Reference Librarian, U.S. Holocaust Memorial Museum (personal communication, March 12, 1998), found the record of David Faber's date of arrival at Auschwitz from his tattoo number in the above reference. Tattoo numbers of prisoners and the associated dates of admission and tattooing were recorded by the Nazis at Auschwitz in their daily records. *Auschwitz Chronicle 1939-1945* is a compilation of documents that includes the tattoo records, which were captured by the Allies after the war. The correct arrival date shows that Faber's time frame at Auschwitz overlaps with that of Mengele, Eichmann, and Fénelon, as he reports. The correct arrival date also shows that Faber's stay in Szebnia, before Auschwitz, was somewhat longer than he recollects, and that his stay at Jawiszowice, after Auschwitz, was somewhat shorter.

Faber reports:

> At the beginning of the war, from 1939 until my family was murdered in the autumn of 1942, I had a good sense of time and dates. But after my family was murdered, and I was alone and taken to Szebnia at the end of 1942, dates become blurred for me. I remember the order of events and the seasons: it was hot in the summer and freezing in the winter. But I am not certain about the exact dates. I was a child, alone in the world, starved, beaten, and terrified, and no one gave us a calendar in the camps. You can change the date [in a subsequent printing of my memoirs], but I will not change what I went through. Changing the date doesn't change anything (David Faber, personal communication, February 27, 1998).

[2] **Dr. Josef Mengele** is well-known for having conducted gruesome experiments on human prisoners, especially at Auschwitz. Like many Nazis, he disappeared after the war, presumably having escaped to South America.

[3] **Fania Fénelon** was a member of the orchestra of women prisoners at Auschwitz. The formal performance area of the orchestra was located at a distance from the gas chamber and not directly in front of it, although Fénelon reports that sometimes members of the orchestra marched around the camp while they played. In his account, Faber conveys the feeling that the orchestra was intimately connected with the gas chamber. Curiously, Fénelon herself describes the orchestra as playing "at the threshold of death" (Fénelon, *Playing for Time*, p. 46-47).

[4] **burned them alive**

The burning of corpses by the Nazis in crematoria and open pits is well known. Less well known is their burning people alive. Other reports of burning alive at Auschwitz include the following:

> These transports were very numerous and it happened that the gas chambers of Crematorium V could not handle everyone. The people for whom there was no more space in the gas chambers were mostly shot by him personally. In many cases he threw living people into the burning pits. [Henryk Tauber, APMO, Höss Trial, vol. 29, p. 47] (Czech, *Auschwitz Chronicle, 1939-1945*, p. 622).

> A huge fire was burning in the distance.... My sister asked a guard who was standing nearby, "What was that noise that was coming from the open fire?" ... The soldier said they were burning cripple

and disabled people ... (Rose Schindler, survivor of Auschwitz, in "Tales of Sorrow and Hope on Yom HaShoah" by Donald Harrison, *San Diego Jewish Press Heritage*, Friday, May 1, 1998, p. 3).

The prisoners barricade themselves in a barn.... The SS men set the barn on fire and murder the prisoners (Czech, p. 726).

Since the wounded are still moving, the SS men bring up several sacks of straw, distribute them in the corners of the barracks, and set everything on fire. Prisoners who attempt to drag themselves from the burning barracks are shot to death... (Czech, p. 803).

[The SS men] set the barracks with all the sick on fire. All prisoners in the prisoners' infirmary barracks die in the flames (Czech, p. 803).

Burning alive by the Nazis in locations other than Auschwitz is also reported, for example:

Ouradour-sur-Glane, French village ... the German soldiers locked 500 women and children in the church and set fire to it... (Zentner and Bedurftig, *The Encylopedia of the Third Reich*, p. 677).

Bialystok, Poland ... The men of Police Battalion 309's First and Third Companies drove their victims in the synagogue.... After spreading gasoline around the building, the Germans set it ablaze.... Between 100 and 150 men of the battalion surrounded the burning synagogue. They collectively ensured that none of the appointed Jews escaped the burning synagogue. They watched as over seven hundred people died this hideous and painful death... (Goldhagen, *Hitler's Willing Executioners*, p. 189-190).

Gardelegen [Germany] ... They chased us all into a large barn.... The Germans poured out petrol and set the barn on fire. Several thousand people were burned alive (Goldhagen, p. 367-370).

[5] **Our toilet was another huge barrack with holes all over the floor.**
    The toilets at Auschwitz were actually latrines. Those that are most familiar from photographs have holes at seat height. However, these photographs do not represent all the latrines.

Who could have dreamed up such a place as that latrine hut? It was an enormous hole dug out of the earth, about forty feet deep, surrounded by an irregular border of large stones, plank walls, and a roof. This enormous, funnel-shaped sewer was ringed with wooden bars.... The smaller ones like me, their legs dangling, had to grip the slippery round bar with both hands with all their might. To fall into the pit must have been a most terrible death (Fénelon, *Playing for Time*, p. 23-24).

Faber reports (personal communication, March 10, 1998) that in the course of his long imprisonment in many concentration camps, he experienced many types of latrines, from the seat types to no latrines at all, the situation at Bergen-Belsen. Fénelon also describes an absence of latrines at Bergen-Belsen:

> The stench was stifling…. They hadn't installed anything approaching latrines … others just let themselves go on the spot (Fénelon, p. 250-251).

Faber reports that even when he had access to the seat type of latrine, he used it like a floor latrine:

> I stood on it [the seat type of latrine] because it was so filthy, covered with urine and feces, that I did not want to sit down on it, and I was too small to squat over it while my feet were on the floor. So I stepped up onto the bench and stood on the latrine seat with my feet straddling the hole, and I squatted up there. The boards were slimy and slippery and the holes were big, and sometimes people fell through the holes (Faber, personal communication, March 10, 1998).

[6] *Sonderkommando*
Special command unit.

CHAPTER 16

[1] **I. G. Farben**
During WWII, I.G. Farben was a synthetic oil and rubber factory at Auschwitz, which used slave labor. ("IG Farben." Encyclopædia Britannica. 2005. Encyclopædia Britannica Online. 25 July 2005 <http://search.eb.com/ eb/article?tocId=9042050&query=I.%20G.%20Farben&ct=>.

CHAPTER 18

[1] **babushkas**
Headscarves traditionally worn by women in Eastern Europe. Also refers to women who wear such headscarves; elderly or peasant women.

CHAPTER 19

[1] **Mikvah**
A ritual purification and cleansing bath that Orthodox Jews take on certain occasions, such as before the Sabbath.

CHAPTER 20

[1] **Krawinkel** (Crawinkel), a subcamp of Buchenwald, was located about 50 miles southwest of Dora-Mittelbau. The distance and location are consistent with Faber's report: "The truck went along a bumpy dirt road for about two hours" between Dora-Mittelbau and Krawinkel (p. 93). The camp appears as "Krawinkel" in the English edition of *The Macmillan Atlas of the Holocaust* (Gilbert, p. 223), as "Crawinkel" in the German edition of the same book, and as "Crawinkel" in the English-language *Historical Atlas of the Holocaust* (United States Holocaust Memorial Mnuseum, p. 147 and 149).

In the 1999 printing of *Because of Romek*, we identified the Krawinkel of Faber's inmprisonment as the Krawinkel forced labor camp in Vollmerhausen (Weinmann, *Das nationalsozialistische Lagersystem (CCP)*, p. 407). However, after the 1999 printing, Brigitte Hallmann, an editor at Deutscher Taschenbuch Verlag (dtv), informed us that she had found a " 'Crawinkel Lager' in the atlas of Martin Gilbert situated near Mittelbau Dora [*sic*]." Hellmann pointed out that this location is more consistent than Vollmerhausen with Faber's report and is therefore the more likely location of his imprisonment (personal communication, November 29, 1999). We confirmed this location as "Krawinkel" in the English edition of Gilbert's atlas, and we agree with Hellmann's conclusion.

CHAPTER 22

[1] **Ohrdruf** is an outlying camp of Buchenwald. Ohrdruf was the first concentration camp to be discovered by American troops, led by General Dwight Eisenhower. David had already been transferred to Bergen-Belsen by this time. It was Eisenhower who ordered military photographers to take pictures of the devastation at Ohrdruf, so as to preserve the evidence of Nazi atrocities.

[2] **Bergen-Belsen**
    David's arrival to Bergen-Belsen from Ohrdruf on March 23, 1945 is confirmed by German transport records (SVG - R.429/Tr.120.234) now held at the Victims of War Service in Belgium. A copy of these transport records are also held at Gedenkstätte Bergen-Belsen, the memorial on the grounds of the camp.

[3] **Typhus** is an infectious disease common in areas where war, famine, or other catastrophes occur. Typhus is characterized by high fever, skin rashes and/or swellings, and severe headache. The disease is spread by lice, ticks, or fleas.

[4] **Mrs. Crosthwaite and Mrs. Montgomery of the British Red Cross**
    The following information is from Mrs. Veronic Marchbanks, Archives Assistant at the British Red Cross:
        Mrs. Margaret Emmeline Montgomery...served at Belsen...[and] was married to a padre who was the brother of Field Marshall

Montgomery. She died in 1993 aged 92 years....

Mrs. Grizel Kinlock Crosthwaire...served as a Welfare Officer in North West Europe from 1944 to 1947.... One of the postings...[was the] Belsen Concentration Camp. After the war, Mrs. Crosthwaite lived in Scotland and became President of the British Red Cross Dumfries Branch. She held this position for over 30 years and then became their patron. Her connection to the British Red Cross continued right up until her death in 1985.

Mrs. Crosthwaite was presented with the MBE (Members of the British Empire) from HM Queen Elizabeth.... She was particularly delighted at this presentation when the Queen recognized her Belsen medal (personal communication, January 17, 1997 through March 19, 1998).

CHAPTER 23

[1] **Anders' Army**

Named after Polish army officer Wladyslaw Anders, who commanded an army of 80,000 men—consisting mainly of Polish prisoners of war and deportees in the Soviet Union. During WWII, Anders' Army fought in the Middle East, and later in Italy against the Germans, under an agreement between the Soviets and the British, who were by this time allies. ("Anders, Wladyslaw." Encyclopædia Britannica. 2005. Encyclopædia Britannica Online. 31 July 2005 <http://search.eb.com/eb/article-9007431>.)

EPILOGUE

[1] **...presumed dead.**

The fate of Otto Grunow is confirmed by a 1997 statement from the Public Records Office in Münster, Germany, as well as a 1963 letter from historian Nehemiah Robinson of the World Jewish Congress.

[2] **...sentenced to death by a Polish court in Tarnów in 1948.**

Rommelmann's fate was confirmed in 1963 by Nehemiah Robinson of the World Jewish Congress. This information was also confirmed in 2004 by the city archives in Tarnów, Poland.

PRONUNCIATION GUIDE

Dombrowa (dom BROH vuh)
Jaso (YAS woh)
Jawiszowice (yah VISH ah vitz)
Katowice (KAT oh vitz eh)
Lwowska (le VOV skuh)
Nowy Sacz (NOH vee sanch)
Pocztowa (put SHTOH vuh)
Pszczyna (ps CHIN uh)
Pustkow (PUST kov)
Sosnowiec (SOS noh vitz)
Szebnia (SHEB nyah)
Szeroka (sheh ROH kuh)
Tarnów (TAR nov)
ulica [street] (oo LEE tsuh)
Walowa (val OH vuh)
Zydowska (zheh DOV skuh)

BIBLIOGRAPHY

Czech, Danuta. *Auschwitz Chronicle* 1939-1945. New York: Henry Holt and Company, Inc., 1990.

Davies, Norman. *God's Playground: A History of Poland in Two Volumes*. Vol. II: *1795 to the Present*. New York: Columbia University Press, 1984.

Encyclopaedia Judaica. Jerusalem, Israel: Keter Publishing House, Ltd., 1971.

Fénelon, Fania. *Playing for Time*. With Marcelle Routier; translated from the French by Judith Landry. New York: Atheneum, 1977.

Gilbert, Martin. *The Macmillan Atlas of the Holocaust*. New York: Macmillan Publishing Companys, Inc., 1982.

Goldhagen, Daniel Jonah. *Hitler's Willing Executioners: Ordinary Germans and the Holocaust*. New York: Vintage Books, 1996.

Gutman, Israel, ed. *Encyclopedia of the Holocaust*. New York: Macmillan Library Reference USA, 1990.

Mokotoff, Gary, and Sallyann Amdur Sack. *Where Once We Walked: A Guide to the Jewish Communities Destroyed in the Holocaust*. Teaneck, NJ: Avotaynu, Inc., 1991.

Musset, Dr. Paul, and Dr. Antonio Lloret. *Concise Encyclopedia of the Atom*. Glasgow: Collins; Chicago: Follet, 1968.

United States Holocaust Memorial Museum. *Historical Atlas of the Holocaust*. New York: Macmillan Publishing USA, 1996.

Weinmann, Martin, comp. *Das nationalsozialistische Lagersystem (CCP)*. With comments by Anne Kaiser and Ursula Krause-Schmitt. Frankfurt am Main: Zweitausendeins, 1990.

Wieczynski, Joseph L., ed. *The Modern Encyclopedia of Russian and Soviet History*. Vol. I. Gulf Breeze, FL: Academic International Press, 1976.

Zentner, Christian, and Friedemann Bedurftig, eds. *The Encyclopedia of the Third Reich*. English translation edited by Amy Hackett. New York: Da Capo Press, 1997.